WORKING WO

How to Make the Impo:

The difference between what's possible and what's not is a construct of the human mind, a matter of perspective, and it's one that can be changed. *Working Wonders* explains the fundamentals that shape the mind: how it builds walls to protect itself and how a person can tear those walls down to tackle challenges that would have previously been discounted as unrealistic. This volume shares case studies featuring people making the impossible a reality and, in doing so, changing the world for the better. On a deeper level and yet still using nontechnical language, the book identifies possible neurological and psychosocial mechanisms that limit the brain, and techniques that may open it up to exploring the seemingly unachievable. Praszkier also introduces the concept of "possibilitivity," a personality trait that reflects the propensity to perceive insurmountable challenges as doable, and concludes by presenting a portfolio of "Do-It-Yourself" techniques.

RYSZARD PRASZKIER is an emeritus professor at the Institute for Social Studies, University of Warsaw, Poland. He has merged decades of practical experience in the field of social innovation with his passion for academic research and connecting theory with practice.

WORKING WONDERS

How to Make the Impossible Happen

RYSZARD PRASZKIER

University of Warsaw

CAMBRIDGE
UNIVERSITY PRESS

CAMBRIDGE
UNIVERSITY PRESS

University Printing House, Cambridge CB2 8BS, United Kingdom

One Liberty Plaza, 20th Floor, New York, NY 10006, USA

477 Williamstown Road, Port Melbourne, VIC 3207, Australia

314–321, 3rd Floor, Plot 3, Splendor Forum, Jasola District Centre, New Delhi – 110025, India

79 Anson Road, #06-04/06, Singapore 079906

Cambridge University Press is part of the University of Cambridge.

It furthers the University's mission by disseminating knowledge in the pursuit of education, learning, and research at the highest international levels of excellence.

www.cambridge.org
Information on this title: www.cambridge.org/9781108428606
DOI: 10.1017/9781108553148

© Cambridge University Press 2019

First published 2019

Printed in the United Kingdom by TJ International Ltd. Padstow Cornwall

A catalogue record for this publication is available from the British Library.

Library of Congress Cataloging-in-Publication Data
Names: Praszkier, Ryszard, 1945– author.
Title: Working wonders : how to make the impossible happen / Ryszard Praszkier, University of Warsaw.
Description: Cambridge, United Kingdom;
New York, NY : Cambridge University Press, 2019. |
Includes bibliographical references and index.
Identifiers: LCCN 2019019446 | ISBN 9781108428606 (hardback) |
ISBN 9781108450720 (paperback)
Subjects: LCSH: Problem solving. | Creative thinking. |
Adaptability (Psychology) | Organizational change. | Social change.
Classification: LCC BF449.P73 2019 | DDC 153.4/3–dc23
LC record available at https://lccn.loc.gov/2019019446

ISBN 978-1-108-42860-6 Hardback
ISBN 978-1-108-45072-0 Paperback

Contents

Figures

vii

Acknowledgments

First and foremost, I want to thank the people who've made the impossible happen and, in doing so, have changed the world for better. They were the core source of knowledge and inspiration for this book.

Much of the impetus for this book came from Ashoka founder and CEO William Drayton and from University of Warsaw Professor Andrzej Nowak, whose insightful observations seeded many of my ideas. It's also a pleasure to thank friends who have been critically important advisors throughout this endeavor. In particular, I am grateful for the mentorship of Zbigniew "Bish" Turlej, Ph.D., a physicist and business analyst, whose healthy skepticism kept me grounded. I thank Professor David Brée, Ph.D., for his diligent cooperation throughout the entire project and his thoughtful comments and feedback.

Many thanks to my son, Tom Praszkier, for his professional help in preparing the photos. Thanks to Helen Taylor for her editorial skills and significant comments and suggestions, which have added value to the content of this publication. I also want to thank Taylor Leet-Otley, the Ashoka volunteer, for ironing out the wrinkles.

Finally, I want to thank my wife, Anna, whose intelligence and constructive criticism served as my guidepost for this and all previous publications. May she rest in peace.

The book is credited to the Robert B. Zajonc Institute for Social Studies, University of Warsaw.

Author's Note
List of Characters

In this book we will present multiple case studies and examples of individuals who, in spite of the prevailing conviction that their vision was impossible to realize, remained confident that it was doable and successfully implemented their ideas. These remarkable people come from different countries and continents around the world, and vary in social strata, education, experience, age, and gender. They include:

Ricardo Semler	Brazil	Chapter 1
Mary Gordon	Canada	Chapter 2
Piotr Pawłowski	Poland	Chapter 3
Shannon Dosemagen	USA	Chapter 4
Arif Khan	Pakistan	Chapter 4
Temp Keller	USA	Chapter 10
Lucy Chagnon	Canada	Chapter 10
Temple Grandin	USA	Chapter 10
Amit Agarwal	India	Chapter 12
Karin Strauss	USA	Chapter 12
Carlos Mario Rodriguez	Costa Rica	Chapter 12
Anna Young	USA	Chapter 12
Brian Bannon	USA	Chapter 12
Dori Roberts	USA	Chapter 12
Gen. Stanley McChrystal	USA	Chapter 13
Karim Sy	Senegal	Chapter 17
Denis Ole Sonkoi	Kenya	Chapter 17
Fr. Paul Okoth	Uganda	Chapter 17
Preeda Limmontakul	Thailand	Chapter 17
Chris Rufer	USA	Chapter 22
Dennis W. Bakke	USA	Chapter 22
Jerry White	USA	Chapter 25

Bart Weetjens	Tanzania	Chapter 25
Elizabeth Fry	Great Britain	Précis
Bill Strickland	USA	Précis
Ndinini Sikar	Tanzania	Précis
Carlo Pertini	Italy	Précis

Introduction

As children, many of us are taught to be realists. We are told that we should stop dreaming, and to keep our heads out of the clouds. We are told that we shouldn't bite off more than we can chew or meddle with things out of our depth. Instead, we are cautioned to cut our coats according to their cloth and hedge our bets.

This book proposes another way to be. It shows that dreaming can be constructive, and that by following our dreams, we can erase the boundaries between what's "realistic" and what's "unrealistic." In her hit song "Impossible," Kelly Clarkson challenges those who would dissuade her from pursuing her dreams and prays to be able to "do the impossible." She sings:[1]

> Can't change the winds, you say
> Won't matter anyway
> Can't reach that far 'cause it's impossible
> It's impossible
> Can't rise above this place
> Won't change your mind so I pray
> Breakin' down the walls
> Do the impossible.

Against all odds, she chooses a "lonely road" to realize her dream:

> Walkin' by myself I know
> This lonely road's becomin' my new home
> But I don't stop, I just keep movin' on.

And finds that what others see as impossible is possible for her:

> It's impossible to you
> Not impossible for me
> Not impossible for me

---

[1] See www.youtube.com/watch?v=jQOnBqycX1c (retrieved March 16, 2019).

Spoke up and thought I'd try
Try to step across the line.

Actually, I could stop right there, as the message of that song and this book are essentially the same. But I want to go deeper. I want to take a closer look at what makes us believe that something's impossible and how to change that belief and make it seem possible.

Of course, many things really are impossible. No one will ever move faster than the speed of light, for example. But our challenge as humans is to distinguish between the two. Hence the Serenity Prayer:[2]

God, grant me the serenity
to accept the things I cannot change,
courage to change the things I can,
and wisdom to know the difference.

This book will help you to identify the difference between the truly impossible and the possible, and to learn how to swim between the two. Why the latter? Because between "truly impossible" and "obviously possible" lies a gray area where something that strikes most people as impossible seems possible for a few.

How we navigate this nebulous space is determined by the mind. Our minds build entrenched and well-fortified fortresses of belief as a form of protection, to safeguard their territory and ward off change. The "magic" of making the impossible possible comes when we transcend the mind's self-imposed limits. Inside the well-protected bastions of our minds are gems of potential waiting to be discovered. My purpose here is to show you what holds us back from achieving big things in life and how you can become one of those "magicians" who make the impossible possible.

Fortunately, we have wonderful examples of individuals who've successfully broken through the fortress walls of the mind and achieved astounding things. Take, for example, Muhammad Yunus, the 2006 Nobel Peace Prize winner who introduced banking for the poor (see Figure 1).[3] To many, the idea that rural Bangladeshi women – the poorest of the poor – could get bank loans and invest in their own businesses sounded silly and naïve.

"Muhammad," everyone said, "are you crazy? How can a bank give loans to people who can't guarantee repayment?" But Yunus ignored his critics and launched a program to provide small loans to groups of five women

---

[2] Written by the American theologian Reinhold Niebuhr.
[3] See www.grameen.com (retrieved March 16, 2019); also Muhammad Yunus's book (2003).

Figure 1 Muhammad Yunus receiving the 2006 Nobel Peace Prize.
Received from the Yunus Center.

each. The group guaranteed the loans, which revolved annually, so that each woman had the opportunity to invest the money in her business for a year and then forward it to the next group member.[4] Within five years, five new businesses would emerge, and the bank would be repaid with interest. Yunus's brilliant idea spread throughout the world and is now commonly known as a micro-loan program.

Yunus is just one example of someone determined to do the "impossible" in order to create opportunity and improve lives. We'll look at several diverse cases of people who, in business, in the social sector, and in their personal lives, overcame the prevailing belief that their dreams were impossible and made those dreams happen.

We'll also look at the "dark" tapestry of forces that reinforces the fortress of the mind. We'll consider the neuroscience involved, including factors that inhibit the brain's natural plasticity. We'll look at powerful psychosocial influences, such as the perceived need to maintain consistency in our thinking by any means necessary and the tendency to give in to the opinion of the majority. And we'll look at the influence of networks on our ability to incorporate new information and ideas.

---

[4] You can see a micro-loan group at www.results.org.au/protect-role-women-in-grameen-bank (retrieved March 16, 2019).

These are the patchwork pieces we stitch together to "protect" ourselves from things we haven't considered, to curb our potential, and to inhibit achievement. With an understanding of these dark forces, we'll turn our attention to the "light" tapestry of forces that helps us overcome the mind's limitations. The basic elements are similar, but they work in opposition. There is the neuroscience component (increasing the brain's plasticity); the psycho-social component (how the minority can influence the majority, and the positive influence of networks through expanded connectivity).

These two tapestries – the dark and the light – continuously operate at cross-purposes within us. Sadly, the dark one typically wins. The fortress of the mind grows over time, making it harder to see opportunities outside of the mainstream. To stay open to possibility and work our magic in the world, we need counter-spells that conjure the light tapestry's magic and break the spell of impossibility. In the final chapters of this book, we'll introduce an array of these "counter-spells." Some involve emotion, some relate to thinking, and some call for physical action. We will even delve into how to use the hidden world of imagination to defeat the dark forces of limitation.

The ground covered in these pages is familiar territory to me. While writing my previous books, *Social Entrepreneurship: Theory and Practice* and *Empowering Leadership of Tomorrow*,[5] I became convinced of the existence of a certain kind of "magic" that controls our beliefs about what is possible and what isn't. As an academician I kept these thoughts in the back of my mind, blending them with my practical experience as a second-opinion reviewer for the Fellowship of Ashoka, Innovators for the Public,[6] a global association that empowers social innovators and entrepreneurs. I've travelled around the world interviewing very special individuals who tackle pressing, though seemingly insurmountable and intractable, social problems. Their work reverses established patterns and introduces systemic, durable change. Each encounter with an Ashoka candidate reminds me that there is something very special happening in the world. Against all odds, and often against the authorities and even their friends and families, these individuals have attempted the "impossible" and "magically" made it possible. You will find in this book many stories of these remarkable people and their astonishing achievements.

It was as an academician, a practitioner, and a writer that I decided to write this book. However, this is not solely an academic endeavor. My aim

---

[5] Praszkier and Nowak (2012); Praszkier (2018).
[6] See www.ashoka.org (retrieved March 16, 2019).

here is to provide a simple and straightforward exploration of the potential each of us has and to provide tips and methods for peeling away self-imposed limitations and unlocking that potential. This book is my way of sharing my fascination with the magic of the mind and my profound belief that this magic is available to all.

Our departure point is a collection of three stories from the business and social sectors. Next, we'll look at the "dark tapestry," followed by mechanisms for overcoming the mind's defenses. Finally, we'll cover a handful of hints and techniques to unleash the mind's creative potential.

One final comment before we take off: The mission of Ashoka, Innovators for the Public is "EACH: Everyone A CHangemaker." My objective here is to make this vision accessible to all and help empower you to pursue your dreams. I remember when I worked with business students, how important this discovery was for them. They believed that choosing a business career meant postponing their youthful dreams. How surprised they were to learn that by revealing and pursuing those dreams, they actually became more effective in business.

I hope that this book will help you make the impossible possible and fulfill your greatest dreams.

PART I

Those Who Made the Impossible Happen

Let's start with some vivid examples of people who have solved insurmountable problems and reached seemingly impossible goals in the business and social sectors as well as in their personal lives. I've chosen these three from among many others who have felt compelled to pursue their impossible dreams in the face of adversity and skepticism.

Many in this group are social entrepreneurs who have become Ashoka Fellows. Since 1980, Ashoka has empowered social innovators in more than 80 countries.[1] As a second-opinion reviewer, I have interviewed more than 100 candidates for the Ashoka Fellowship. They have come from Maasai nomadic tribes in Kenya and Tanzania, from high in the Himalayas in Nepal, from rural and urban communities in Pakistan, and from all possible walks of life in India. They've struggled with constraints in Venezuela, built peace in Nigeria and the Middle East, supported emigrants from Syria, empowered small family farmers in Egypt, supported affordable housing in Mexico, raised the educational level in American inner cities, and more.

Add to this remarkable group any number of innovative business-people whose "odd" ideas were met with skepticism but who persisted in the face of criticism and ultimately succeeded in making the "aberration" the trend. And finally, there are those who've faced daunting personal challenges, yet were able to realize their dreams under seemingly impossible conditions.

We'll share some of their stories later in the book, but let's begin with these three examples of extraordinary vision and persistence.

---

1 For the impact of Ashoka see Wells (2018).

CHAPTER I

"The Purpose of Work Is to Feel Good about Life"

At one time Ricardo Semler, the unlikely hero of this story, preferred playing guitar to working in business. But with all the focus and tenacity it takes to become a great musician, Ricardo achieved the "impossible," turning a struggling family business into a thriving company with revenue in excess of $200 million and creating a management style now in use across the globe.

Pursuing a New Idea against All Odds

Brazil, in the early 1970s, was run by a military dictatorship. Not surprisingly, an autocratic, top-down management style was predominant in the private sector as well. The Semler Company was a prime example.[1] Established in 1954 by Antonio Curt Semler, who was then the CEO, the company was faltering in a changing market. When Antonio invited his son Ricardo, then 20 years old, to help run the company, it was in dire straits financially.

Young Ricardo, who was more interested in playing guitar in a rock band, was reluctant to join the family business. Only when the promise of a career in music faded did he agree to come on board. He immediately saw that the company was sluggish, due largely to a host of managers entrenched in their old routines. In short order he proposed several substantial changes he believed would make the firm more resilient. Antonio opposed them, prompting heated clashes between father and son. But despite a torrent of criticism from his father and the threatened managers, Semler clung to his vision of the workplace as a nimble and agile society of coworkers. At one point he even threatened to leave the company. Antonio, rather than see that happen, resigned in 1980 and transferred majority ownership to his son. Semler was 21 years old and full of energy

---

[1] Based on Fisher (2005); Maresco and York (2005); Hamel (2007); Daft (2015).

and vision for a much more democratic and responsive working environment. On his first day as CEO, he fired 60 percent of all top managers and began work on a diversification program to rescue the company.

Semler's cardinal vision was to give voice to coworkers and enable their initiative. To that end he changed the name of the company to SEMCO Partners[2] and accepted a proposal from three of his engineers to set up a new unit to identify new initiatives. The Nucleus of Technological Innovation (NTI) soon started bubbling with new ideas, one of which was to make the company's engineers partners and shareholders, thereby tying their pay directly to the results of their work. This initiative became a template for other satellite units created throughout the company. The number of employees in each of these satellite units was limited to 150–200, so that everyone in a unit could get to know each other and form a community with a common purpose. By the late 1980s, two-thirds of the company's workforce and products were in these satellite units.

Over the years, SEMCO also adopted the idea of autonomous teams. Teams began hiring and firing workers and supervisors through a voting process, and policy manuals were replaced with a policy of common sense. In fact, the only actual manual, which runs to merely about 20 pages, is filled with cartoons.

Semler stayed true to his vision of a friendly community at work. He said that the company should be like a village, and in this spirit he broke traditional rules and gradually eliminated the corporate drill: time clocks, dress codes, security procedures, privileged office spaces and perks all disappeared. Semler drove huge change based on a simple, rhetorical question: If people are responsible adults at home, why do we suddenly treat them as adolescents with no freedom when they reach the workplace?

During this period of transformation, SEMCO and its employees thrived. But big change is hard work, and Semler, believing that his continuous engagement was essential to the success of his ideas, had pushed himself to the point of exhaustion. In 1984, while touring a pump factory near New York, he collapsed on the shop floor. The doctor declared him essentially healthy but mentally more strained than any person of that age he had ever seen. After that scare, Semler resolved to harmonize his work life with his personal life and, similarly, to help his employees refashion their lives. The pivotal shift was to consider work as a way to enjoy life. He determined that the purpose of work isn't to make money – it's to make workers feel good about life.

---

[2] See www.semco.com.br/en/ (retrieved March 16, 2019).

Many around him were convinced that this free-spirited management style would lead to the collapse of the company. But Semler stayed the course. "No one works for money alone," he would say. So it was essential to tap into what people wanted from their careers and what they had to offer. To counter his critics he used humor and paradox. He would say, for example, that the key to good management is to get rid of the managers!

He proved to be absolutely right. Under his leadership SEMCO went from near bankruptcy to $4 million in annual revenue in eight years. By 1994, its revenue was $35 million. These were heady times, but the real test of Semler's vision came during the economic crisis in 1998–99. The Brazilian economy spiraled downward, forcing many companies to declare bankruptcy. Unemployment rose from 6 percent before 1998 to 14 percent. In 1999, Brazil owed 46 percent of its GDP to foreign creditors and depleted its reserves in order to finance the deficit, while the Brazilian currency was significantly devalued.

And what happened at SEMCO during this time? Workers demonstrated shared responsibility and agreed to wage cuts of up to 40 percent. They were also given the right to approve every expenditure. Semler created self-managed teams of six to eight workers who were in charge of all aspects of production. They set their own budgets and goals and agreed to tie compensation to budget and productivity. As a result, costs went down and profits went up. Additionally, the defect rate for manufactured products fell below 1 percent.

While many companies were bankrupted during the crisis, SEMCO used this miserable period to create the conditions for post-crisis development. For example, during the crisis, workers performed multiple roles, which gave them greater knowledge of various company operations and strengthened their identification with the company. Ricardo also solicited bottom-up ideas on how to improve the business. After the Brazilian crisis was over, SEMCO's productivity and profit dramatically improved, with revenue rising to $212 million annually in 2002. Its employee count went from 90 in 1982 to 3,000 in 2003.

The Implementation and the Success

SEMCO's spectacular growth-curve (to revenues of $400 million in 2016) gained plenty of public attention. *Time* magazine featured Semler among its profiles of Global 100 young leaders in 1994. The World Economic Forum named him as one of the Global Leaders of Tomorrow. The *Wall Street Journal's* Latin American magazine named him Latin

American Businessman of the Year in 1990 and 1992. And *Turning Your Own Table*, his first book (in Portuguese), became the bestselling non-fiction book in the history of Brazil. Semler has since written two books in English on the transformation of SEMCO and workplace re-engineering. *Maverick* (an English version of *Turning Your Own Table*) was published in 1993, and *The Seven-Day Weekend* came out in 2003 and became an international bestseller. He's also written several articles and made many speeches and is a guest lecturer at Harvard Business School and MIT.[3]

What Are His Messages?

Semler posits that the main objective of granting employees autonomy is to spur their creativity. His groundbreaking insight is that being self-driven increases the propensity to innovate. He also believes that processes and procedures that encumber creativity should be eliminated. For example, in order to remove possible obstacles to innovation, one of SEMCO's norms is that employees have to confine all their circulars, reports, letters, and minutes to a single piece of paper.

Semler endorses responsibility, but not in a pyramidal hierarchy. He sees these pyramids as the cause of much corporate evil, because the tip is too far from the base. Pyramidal structures emphasize power, promote insecurity, distort communications, clog interactions, and make it very difficult for the people who plan and the people who execute to move in the same direction. Instead, the SEMCO organizational model comprises three concentric circles: one corporate level and two operating levels at the manufacturing units. The central circle contains five "Counselors" who integrate the company's movements. Semler is one of them, and with the exception of a few legal documents that refer to him as "President," Counselor is the only title he uses. A second, larger circle contains eight division heads, known as "partners." The third, outermost circle includes all other employees, most of whom are referred to as "Associates." This circular model fosters both horizontal and diagonal communication, which together animate people's creativity.

This model also affords extraordinary freedom to company employees. Semler doesn't believe that control is advantageous. In one of his public presentations, he said that he doesn't care where people work, be it in one of the company's many locations or even at home. He speaks proudly of

---

[3] See, for example, Semler (1994, 1995, 2004).

factory-floor flextime, self-set salaries, unregulated business travel, and a rotating CEO-ship, believing that the returns from trusting people are much higher than the costs and consequences of controlling them.

People who are trusted are more co-responsible, he says. They identify with the company and internalize its goals, becoming reliable partners. In his book, *The Seven-Day Weekend*, he suggests that future managers should enable employees to blend work life and personal life with enthusiasm and creative energy, saying that smart bosses realize an employee might be most productive if they work on Sunday afternoon, play golf on Monday morning, go to a movie on Tuesday afternoon, and watch their child play soccer on Thursdays.

Semler's revolutionary take on business goes beyond creating new operational and organizational models; he has also re-envisioned the definition of success. He thinks little of strategic planning and vision, calling them "barriers to success," and paradoxically disputes the value of growth. A company's success can't be measured in numbers, he claims, since numbers ignore what the end user really thinks of the product and what the people who produce it really think of the company.

Spreading the Word despite Adversity

Given his success, it was natural for Semler to want to share what was working well at SEMCO with others and so he spread the good news to other organizations. His efforts, however, were met with criticism, just as his ideas for the company had been years before. But he was once again determined to make the "undoable" doable. A first step was to address two "myths" (as he called them) about democratic management:

The first myth is that Semler's ideas, while beautiful, are utopian, naïve, and not applicable elsewhere. Semler points out that those ideas took flight not only at SEMCO, but also in many other companies, such as Morning Star, Buurtzorg, Gore-Tex, Netflix, Basecamp, and Buffer.

The second myth is that this approach creates anarchy and fosters insubordination and lack of respect for the leaders, allowing people do whatever they want. Semler responds that when adults are treated with the respect and trust they believe they deserve, and when they feel like they're working toward a greater purpose, they're able to self-organize and decide how to get things done effectively.

In response to the false notion that Semler's ideas couldn't work for large multinationals as they did for small companies, Semler notes that large organizations ultimately comprise many smaller teams, and are well-suited for his management style.[4]

Other naysayers argue that, while Semler's approach might have worked in the 1980s and 1990s, businesses face different challenges today. However, Semler insists that current organizational issues are similar in essence to those from 30 years ago, including remote work, tribal issues, dress codes, and the dissolution of boundaries between personal and professional lives. The way humans work has not changed dramatically, so democratic management hasn't become outdated.

Others chide that if people decide their own salaries, overheads will become too expensive. Semler's answer is that when salary information is shared openly, it's much easier to determine the right compensation and cost structures. Consequently, teams become more aware of expenses, especially when they're working to increase general profitability.

All in all, Semler believes that the philosophy of making people co-responsible is helpful in most settings. Organizations that trap their employees in rigid structures and controls and limit them to doing only what they're told stifle their workers' creativity, cloud their self-identity, and dampen their potential.

In his typical, indefatigable style Semler has taken his ideas to the public, giving speeches, TED talks, and lectures at leading universities, and writing articles and books. This, however, was not enough for him. To better promote the notion of organizing around people instead of policies and procedures, he founded the Semco Style Institute. The Institute puts individuals above organizational modes, treats adults like adults, and sees freedom and self-interest as the basis for collective alignment. Its five pivotal principles are to stimulate trust, self-management, extreme stakeholder alignment, and creative innovation, and to reduce controls.

Semco Style Institute offers a master's program in building organizations that show agility, stimulate performance, and foster entrepreneurship. The Institute also facilitates a leadership program and an experience-exchange program with other similar projects.

And it doesn't stop there. Semler's team has also launched an online gateway called LeadWise[5] for leaders who want to transform their organizations to People-Centric Management. This dialogue-based

---

[4] See https://journal.leadwise.co/10-myths-about-democratic-management-by-ricardo-semler-cf41175 d3cdb (retrieved March 17, 2019).

[5] See www.leadwise.co (retrieved March 16, 2019).

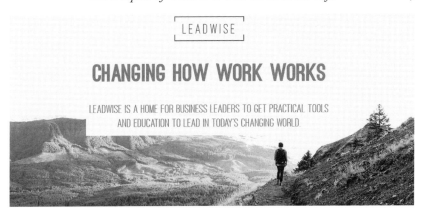

Figure 2 LeadWise home page.
Permission received from LeadWise Institute.

platform offers a full array of webinars, newsletters, podcasts, and programs to teach and spread Semler's demonstrated vision (see Figure 2).

Changing Impossible to Possible

When Ricardo Semler took over his father's firm at 21, his ideas looked unworkable and naïve to many. But something inside of him told him otherwise. What was it that propelled him forward in the face of skepticism and scorn to achieve so much? We'll soon answer that, but first let's meet anther remarkable individual determined to achieve the "impossible."

CHAPTER 2

Bringing Empathy to Schools

Aggression and Bullying in Schools Become Prevailing

In the 1970s a young Canadian named Mary Gordon graduated from college and became a kindergarten teacher, in the hope that she could have a positive effect on children's lives. She hadn't been teaching long when she became very concerned about the aggression and bullying she witnessed in class. In a typical instance, one boy grabbed a hat from another boy's head, in front of the other kids. The victim immediately became the target of ridicule from his classmates, and to Mary, it was obvious that he felt intimidated and helpless. Fortunately, a 10-year-old boy named Jessie stepped forward and told the bully to give the hat back. The bully, seeing the other kids begin to side with the victim, complied. It had taken Jessie's boldness and compassion to bring about a positive end to an all too familiar event that often leaves the victims feeling mocked and abased.

Mary Gordon found that bullying in schools was on the rise and had damaging effects. Bullying is not only traumatic for the victim but also has long-term consequences for the perpetrator. Research has shown that students who are bullies early in school are more prone to aggressive behavioral problems and violence, frequent school absence or dropping out, low grades, and even juvenile delinquency. Some studies also indicate that early school bullying may lead to more serious violent behaviors including using a weapon, frequent fighting, and fighting-related injury.

Much has been done to try to reduce school bullying, but results have been modest at best. Increasing control may only push bullying into the shadows, making it less conspicuous but still present. Lecturing and persuasion have also yielded little improvement. Indeed, it's been difficult for researchers to find and document any positive results from programs designed to prevent aggression in schools. Bullying became perceived as inevitable, and to some extent it is and will remain so.

A Dream: School Without Aggression

But not for Gordon. She became obsessed with trying to prevent aggression in early school years. But how was she to curb the grabbing of hats and the ensuing ridicule? How was she to encourage more "Jessies" to intervene? How was she to spark compassion and understanding?

Her first step was to focus on her preschoolers' families, especially families who were failing to provide loving, supportive relationships. Through this work she gained an appreciation of the importance of family in a child's life. And that led her to found Canada's first Parenting and Family Literacy Centers in 1981. At these centers, situated predominantly in low-income districts, Gordon invited groups of parents to share with one another their experiences, their problems and potential solutions to those problems. This wasn't a place for preaching or telling parents what they should do. It was a caring environment, a safe space where stressed parents could get things off their chest and find help. At Gordon's centers, parents also had the opportunity to talk with their children's preschool teachers, to find out how their kids were doing and address problematic behavior.

Gordon took to the streets to get folks involved, engaging them in laundromats, diners, wherever they gathered. The program grew steadily over two decades, reaching the deepest inner-city schools with the highest dropout and teen pregnancy rates to help children find a better future. Gordon's work is legendary, and her program is internationally recognized and continues to this day.

The Key to Change in the Classroom

While Gordon's Parenting and Family Literacy Centers provided invaluable support to many families and children, the programs didn't address the bullying she'd witnessed in the kindergarten classrooms where she taught. Gordon continued to ask herself what, if anything, might make a real difference. Her answer: *empathy*.

It was empathy for the boy who lost his hat that prompted Jessie to intervene and force the bully to give it back. Empathy lets us step into another's shoes to not only understand how that person feels, but also to have those same feelings ourselves. Gordon determined that the way to end bullying was to encourage empathy in schools as early as possible, when the children's brains are plastic and more receptive to understanding and feeling the feelings of others.

But how to do it? How do you introduce the concept of empathy to children in a meaningful way? The general opinion was that it was hopeless; aggression had always been a part of us and always would be. Most kindergarten teachers even believed that aggression was a natural human behavior that kids were destined to explore in their earlier years. Gordon, however, believed that behavior could be changed and that there must be a way to do it. She believed that people simply underestimate children's ability to act for good, and that there's a benevolence in children that could be brought to the fore.

Gordon found her answer to "how" when she noted that many of her students' mothers came to the school with babies in their arms and observed the children's reaction to the infants. It dawned on her that by observing a baby's emotions, children could learn about their own emotions and about the emotions of others. The trusting and helpless baby triggers curiosity: Why does he smile or cry? How can I appease or entertain him? If contact with babies could help teach these kids to feel what others feel, Gordon thought, then why not bring them into the classroom?

Baby Time

In 1966, Gordon's brilliant idea to eradicate bullying and introduce empathy took shape as the Roots of Empathy (ROE) program.[1] She invited neighborhood mothers to bring their babies to class, where the infants would become the teachers. The children sang to the babies, touched and talked to them, and asked the mothers questions. Then they talked about their experience with a ROE instructor. Eventually, ROE moved beyond kindergarten, as well-organized programs developed for children in grades 1–3 and 4–6. ROE instructors meet with a class before and after each family visit for a total of 27 sessions. And it works!

Even the most rambunctious class quiets down when a mother and baby arrive. The students stand in a circle and greet the baby with a song; one I recorded went, "Hi, baby Dustin, how are you? How are you? How are you? Hi, baby Dustin, how are you? How are you today?" As they sing the mother makes a round, introducing the baby closely to each student.

Next the children sit in a circle, and the mother places the baby on a blanket in the middle. The children – even those who are the most talkative, overactive, and aggressive – sit quietly and observe, ask questions,

---

[1] See Gordon (2005); www.ashoka.org/en/fellow/mary-gordon#intro (retrieved March 16, 2019); also based on my interview with Mary Gordon, April 24, 2017.

and gently touch or rock the baby. And, magically, bullies turn into nice guys (see Figure 3).

In the years since she started the ROE program, Gordon has collected many stories of remarkable transformation. There's the one about Darren, a school bully who'd been held back twice, until he was two years older than his classmates. When Darren was four he witnessed his mother being killed, and he'd been living in foster homes ever since. He played the tough guy at school, adopting a menacing demeanor intended to intimidate. But during a session with the baby something softened inside him. He volunteered to hold the baby, went to a quiet corner and rocked him. At some point he asked the instructor, "If nobody ever loved you, do you think you could still be a good father?"

Darren's experience allowed him to open up and accept his own feelings, which changed him dramatically. Another student, named David, was an isolated autistic boy whom the other kids didn't want to socialize with. After the baby-in-the-classroom experience, David's classmates were more understanding. They could empathize with his feelings of isolation and they began to include him. David was invited to parties and made many friends – social connections that improved his life immensely.

Not surprisingly, Gordon's ideas were initially met with resistance and doubt – a common response to innovation, especially within the school system. First, there were legal concerns: Would the school be liable if a student accidently, or even intentionally, hurt a baby? Gordon researched the issue and determined that the mother's presence absolved the schools of legal responsibility. A waiver was developed to further clarify the matter.

Also of concern was the mothers' availability. When the program began maternity leave in Canada was limited to three months. Working mothers simply couldn't participate in a nine- or 10-month program. Gordon solved this by going directly to the employers. In most cases they agreed to give the mothers flexibility to participate in the program during working hours. Merrill Lynch, for example, gave every employee with a baby full permission to be a ROE parent. Gordon also lobbied the Canadian government for extended maternity leave, successfully increasing it to one year.

Another issue was whether such intense focus by a group might harm a baby's psyche. Mary invited more than a dozen prominent pediatric psychiatrists to discuss the matter, and their conclusion was in favor of the program.

One question remained about whether or not close contact between the kids and the baby would enable germ transfer and infections. Gordon

Figure 3 Roots of Empathy: the baby becomes the teacher.
Received from Mary Gordon, Founding President of Roots of Empathy.

immediately consulted pediatricians who said it was fine, especially since the mother controls the scope of physical contact. Moreover, the children and mother agree beforehand how much interaction they can have with the baby. And the kids wash their hands before the visit. Gordon even invited a preeminent North American epidemiologist to sit on the board of ROE.

The teachers' union also had concerns. They weren't keen on having someone who wasn't a teacher (namely, the ROE instructor) come into the classroom and do a teacher's job. But Gordon was able to convince the unionists that the program wouldn't infringe on teachers' rights, and a final endorsement from the Teachers' Federation to the Ontario government was a great step forward.

Some school authorities claimed that ROE was taking time from mathematics and other lessons. In response Gordon pointed out that children need to feel relaxed, happy, open, and understood to be able to learn, and her program accomplished that. ROE not only builds emotional literacy so that children understand their feelings and have the vocabulary to talk about them, it also creates a risk-free learning zone, where no one will laugh at you or make fun of you and whatever you have to say will be listened to and taken seriously. This kind of environment not only made kids happier and kinder, it made them smarter, as shown by their improved scores in mathematics and English.

Documenting ROE's Impact

Despite the school system's initial reluctance to try something new, the ROE program eventually spread to many schools in and around Toronto. Gordon gathered more stories of school bullies' "magical" transformations into empathetic kids, and the program's growing popularity led her to another turning point. Why not take it to a broader audience, she wondered? Why not bring empathy to other Ontario schools? Or to all of Canada?

At this point the goals of the program were clear: to develop children's social and emotional understanding, to promote prosocial behavior while decreasing aggression, and finally, to increase children's knowledge about infants, human development, and parenting. The power of ROE to accomplish these things in the short term was evident. But skeptics wanted proof of longer-lasting change in the children. Gordon understood that to convince academic authorities of the program's success and to ensure that it continued to spread, she needed hard evidence demonstrating that the impact was sustainable. But how could she prove that the change in Darren after he rocked the baby would last? That he would no longer be aggressive, wouldn't drop out of school, and wouldn't get into drugs as an adolescent? It was another challenge that seemed impossible to many, but not to Gordon.

It was around 2000 when she decided to team up with universities to carry out meticulous research on the issue, in which classes participating in ROE were matched with similar classes that weren't. The results showed that children who participated in the program demonstrated:[2]

- increased social and emotional knowledge;
- decreased aggression;
- increased prosocial behavior (e.g., sharing, helping, and including);
- increased perceptions of the classroom as a caring environment;
- increased understanding of infants and parenting.

To demonstrate the durability of these results, Gordon worked with the government of Manitoba to launch a research project in 2001 that measured changes in students directly after and again three years after a ROE experience. Results showed a significant increase in prosocial behavior and decrease in aggression – both immediately after the program and three years later. The Manitoba government was so impressed that it now supports broad implementation of the program, including in First Nation and remote fly-in communities.

With proof of ROE's long-term efficacy in hand, nothing could stop Gordon from taking it far and wide. Today ROE is offered in almost every Canadian province and is also practiced in the United States, Great Britain, Ireland, Switzerland, Germany, New Zealand, Japan, and many other countries.

Now the Preschoolers!

Mary Gordon's story could have ended here, but of course it doesn't. Instead, she has continued to explore the "impossible." She was convinced that the earlier children learn empathy, the more lasting it becomes, as the younger brain is more receptive and easily changes. So she set out to bring empathy training to toddlers three to five years old. Undaunted by the challenge of teaching children so young, she introduced the Seeds of Empathy (SOE) project in 2005. Neighborhood families bring their babies

---

[2] Santos et al. (2011); Schonert-Reichl et al. (2012).

to specially designed centers where trained Family Guides encourage the young participants to observe the baby's development, name the baby's emotions, and talk about their own feelings and those of others. The program also includes stories to help children explore their own feelings and consider the perspective of others. Specially trained Literacy Coaches facilitate storytelling and discussion in Literacy Circles that help shape early attitudes toward reading. SOE also has a training element to prepare preschool teachers to facilitate similar programs on their own.

Changing Impossible to Possible

Eradicating bullying from schools seemed an impossible task, but Gordon envisioned school as a place for nurturing empathy, not spawning aggression. Her passion and creativity helped her overcome every obstacle, against all odds and despite heavy skepticism, to develop a game-changing program, document its lasting results, and spread it across Canada and around the world.[3] Then, as if that weren't enough, she did the same for preschool children. For these remarkable achievements Mary Gordon won in May 2018 the prestigious Ontario Governor General's Innovation Award.

Hey, Mary, what's next?

---

[3] A four-minute BBC video highlighting ROE is available at www.youtube.com/watch?reload= 9&v=TH5mmBEMavI (retrieved March 16, 2019).

CHAPTER 3

"Moving the World with One Hand"

I first visited Piotr Pawłowski when he was preparing his Ashoka candidacy in 1995. He was lying in bed, paralyzed after breaking his spine. I sat and listened for hours as he told me the sad story of his injury and how he decided to use his unfortunate experience as a warning for others. Over several years I closely observed the rapid development of his social endeavor to make the world a better place for the disabled. We met several times, and I feel privileged to say that we became friends. Here is his story.

Disaster Strikes

As a teenager Piotr was a promising basketball player. He trained intensively in the sport he loved, but also found time to hang out with friends, go to rock concerts, date girls, and generally enjoy life. In 1982, when he was 16, he dove into a shallow river and broke his fourth and fifth cervical vertebrae. The incident left him paralyzed with only limited use of one hand.

After several operations and hospital-based rehab, he was still confined to a bed – not even able to use a wheelchair. Now completely dependent on his parents, he had no hope of completing high school or pursuing his university dreams. His friends and girlfriend gradually stopped visiting him.

Piotr remembers this period as a black hole of depression and hopelessness. He felt lonely, dependent, and useless. Leaving his apartment was a true challenge, not only because there were very few accommodations for the disabled in Poland at the time, but also because he was embarrassed by people's comments and curious looks. A disabled person on the street attracted attention, and Piotr's humiliation was acute when, as his father lifted him from his wheelchair and put him in the car, children gathered around to gawk and whisper. So he retreated into a life of isolation, comforting himself with television and food and slipping deeper into a profound depression.

First Glimmers of Hope

At some point during this dark period he encountered a book written by Joni Eareckson Tada, a wheelchair-bound woman who traveled around the world giving hope to the disabled by encouraging them to thank God for what they had, instead of dwelling on what they'd lost.[1] Piotr met Joni when she visited Poland and was so inspired that he decided to change his life. First he learned to write using his mouth to hold a pen. Writing opened an avenue to connect with people and share his thoughts. For the first time he felt some optimism. When he met disabled people who painted by holding a brush with their mouths or feet, he was amazed with the quality of their paintings and soon mastered mouth-painting himself. His sketches were good enough to be exhibited and find buyers (see Figure 4).[2]

Buoyed by his progress, Piotr decided to complete high school, with a focus on learning English. Soon he began giving English lessons in order to support himself. He went to college, received a graduate degree and even started a Ph.D. program, though he withdrew because he was too busy with his other activities. As his confidence grew, he also started meeting with new friends. Initially he would go out only in the evenings, so as to be less visible. But gradually he shed his shyness and ventured out during the day as well.

Making It About Others

While participating in rehab programs, Piotr met and socialized with others who were disabled. During one such encounter, in 1992, he got into conversation with a young man about what they could do next. They came up with the idea of a Polish magazine for the disabled, and as their enthusiasm grew, they agreed on the title *Integration* and decided to launch the concept.[3]

Not surprisingly, skeptics weighed in: "You're both in wheelchairs; aren't you biting off more than you can chew?" they wondered. But Piotr and

---

[1] Eareckson-Tady (1980).
[2] Photos from Association Integration.
[3] Based on Pawłowski (2009); Ashoka webpage: www.ashoka.org/en/fellow/piotr-pawlowski#fellow-accordion (retrieved March 16, 2019); also based on my interview with Piotr Pawłowski on April 26, 2017.

Figure 4   Piotr Pawłowski's mouth-paintings.
Received from Integration Association.

his partner would not be dissuaded. Working from Piotr's apartment with the help of volunteers and a print shop that agreed to donate paper and printing, they brought the magazine to life. Piotr initially supported the endeavor with income from English lessons and paintings he had sold, but almost instantly *Integration* received a cascade of letters from various institutions and donors offering support. Between 2009 and 2016, the magazine grew from 8 pages to 16, then to 32, 48, 64, and finally to 92 pages, with 30,000–50,000 copies sold bimonthly.

In 1995, Piotr and his friends decided to register the Friends of Integration Association, to serve as an umbrella organization for their multiple initiatives. In short order, Piotr, together with a trendy pop band, launched a dramatic TV spot to warn against diving into unknown water. Air time was donated by Polish TV channels, and the ad, shown far and wide, had a significant preventive impact. In 1999, Friends of Integration launched a national billboard campaign to raise awareness of disabilities and the need for accessibility. Along highways, in cities, at railway stations, nearly everywhere, one could see these signs with the striking images of famous sculptures missing an arm or leg to symbolize the plight of the disabled. In 2003, during the European Year of People with Disabilities, the group came up with an even stronger national campaign. Five TV spots each presented a different disability and asked the question: "Are we really so different?" These five sketches were also placed on multiple billboards in a campaign that reached millions of Poles and influenced countless minds.

Business was booming, and Piotr's personal circumstances continued to improve. In 1999, he married his love, Ewa, who was his collaborator on Friends of Integration, a friend and a great supporter. Ewa now works as a nurse-midwife but continues to support her husband's efforts with joy and optimism.

Skepticism

Even with universal support, Piotr's work would not have been easy. And at each stage he encountered ample skepticism. When he started, most couldn't believe that someone who could move only one hand could improve accessibility for Poland's disabled citizens and remove the stigma of disability in Polish culture. "What you desire is impossible, young man," Piotr often heard. But time and again he has proved his skeptics wrong, as he continues to achieve his dreams. Even today Friends of Integration continues to grow, having an impact on more than two million people in 2017, influencing Polish attitudes toward disabilities and the attitudes of the disabled toward their own activities. But perhaps the biggest impact has been the most tangible: changes to the design of public and residential buildings to better accommodate the disabled – an accomplishment that also helped secure the organization's financial future.

Building Sustainability

Because of its impact, the Friends of Integration Association gained recognition as a leading non-governmental organization. However, as with most NGOs, funding was donation based, mostly in the form of grants from socially responsible businesses or government agencies. This dependency made for a very tight and unstable budget, affecting staff turnover. Piotr knew independent funding was preferable, so he turned his focus to the organization's economic sustainability and stability. This opened a veritable Pandora's box of criticism and doubt: "How can a group of disabled people generate their own revenue, cover their costs and generate enough profit to support their mission?" "Other well-known NGOs with able-bodied leaders couldn't make it and are still supported by donations, so aren't you daydreaming?" "You need to be realistic and face facts."

But Piotr was unfazed. By 2016, Friends of Integration had achieved financial sustainability. Naysayers were astonished. "How did he do it," they wondered? "How are they making money?"

Well, first they created market demand. For years they'd been building awareness around the issue of accessibility, not just in terms of the way buildings and public spaces were designed, but also in the field of electronics and software applications – making these accessible for people with vision or hearing impairments. As accessibility became a must-have among architects, whether of buildings or software, the organization was in an ideal position to help these professionals address the emerging needs of the market.

At this point the solution was simple: Friends of Integration created a business venture to offer consulting services to web content providers and application producers, as well as to designers and architects. The venture accomplished two things: It generated enough revenue to make Friends of Integration no longer dependent on capricious donors, enabling more investment in their own endowment. And it supported the organization's overarching mission to improve accessibility for the disabled.

This innovative approach to self-sustainability raised more than a few eyebrows, as some wondered whether an organization operating in the social realm had what it took to compete in the business world. But that only made Piotr more determined to succeed.

Changing Impossible to Possible

After Piotr suffered his devastating injury, simply leaving the house seemed an insurmountable task. But he had within him what it took to reclaim his life and make the "impossible" possible, forever changing the lives of Poland's disabled.

CHAPTER 4

Those Who Made the Impossible Happen
Drawing Conclusions

What Do They Have in Common?

Ricardo, Mary, and Piotr are, beyond any doubt, Working Wonders. While they faced different challenges, their stories have much in common. They all had a clear *passion and commitment* that kept them on track and wouldn't let them rest until they'd overcome every obstacle they encountered. They're all creative, both in terms of their ability to shape a unique vision that fosters innovation and their knack for finding clever ways to solve and/or circumvent problems and inspire others. And they share a few characteristics common among successful leaders. For example, each has a *high degree of trust* – trusting employees to share responsibilities, or trusting students to take proper care of a baby. They each *believe in the malleability of people and the world*,[1] which makes them *optimistic* and *ready to take reasonable risk*. And each has a strong *individual support network*, avoiding the Lone Ranger approach and staying open to *cooperation*. Finally, they all are resilient, with strong *mechanisms for coping with adversity*.

A New Personality Characteristic: Possibilitivity

In addition to all of those fine qualities, Ricardo, Mary, and Piotr demonstrate yet another key characteristic: They see challenges and obstacles as something to overcome, and they believe in do-ability against all odds. They believe that a company can be profitable when employees are given the power to co-decide and be co-responsible, that aggression can be eradicated from schools by leveraging empathy and, even more breathtaking, that a baby can be a teacher; and that even with a serious disability of one's own, one can change society's treatment of disabilities.

---

[1] Dweck (2006).

This perception of things as achievable when others see them as unrealizable struck me as a very special personality trait. (Remember Kelly Clarkson's song? "Breakin' down the walls, do the impossible" and "It's impossible to you, not impossible for me.") But the concept felt elusive, and I wrestled with what to call the phenomenon of perceiving challenges as doable. Ultimately I settled on the neologism "possibilitivity" (echoing the pronunciation of "realizability" or "creativity") to describe this quality that I believe each of us has to one degree or another.

Yes, I strongly believe that possibilitivity is a cardinal property of human beings. Since the dawn of man, we've had to instinctively evaluate whether something was worth a try or not. Is this mammoth worth hunting or should we run? Some in the tribe might go after the giant beast, while others, deeming their weapons insufficient, might pass. We're not talking about simply being bold and pursuing the mammoth regardless of the risk; we're considering the way individuals evaluate a situation as hopeless or as promising and worth risk-taking.

In many cases the situation will present an obvious choice. If you're trekking in the mountains and notice a sudden change in the weather, you're smart to conclude that going farther is too risky (undoable), and it's better to return to the nearest shelter. Those who take the risk and continue may put their lives in danger.

Similarly it seems obvious to take action when a group can cooperate to control a threat. Say there is a hooligan in the neighborhood partying late into the night, playing loud music, smashing empty bottles. Teaming up, the neighbors might plan vigils and put pressure on the offender. Obviously, taking action makes a lot of sense in this case.

However, in many situations the decision on whether to take action or not is not so obvious. Some challenges seem undoable on their face, such as a community's challenge to recover from the catastrophic Deepwater Horizon oil spill in the Gulf of Mexico in 2010. In the aftermath of the disaster, it seemed that the oil company and remediation agencies were slow to take action or simply not able to oversee all aspects of the recovery. The affected community could either passively observe as the oil slick continued to spread and threaten their home, or they could take action. Typically the process to monitor the slick would require very expensive and complicated equipment. With those resources out of reach, one might expect that the task would be deemed futile, and the community would remain wholly at the mercy of the oil company.

But Shannon Dosemagen[2] was undaunted. She produced her own "open technology" monitoring equipment out of old cameras attached to

---

[2] See www.ashoka.org/fellow/shannon-dosemagen (retrieved March 16, 2019).

balloons or kites and trained citizens to monitor the damage themselves. Working to increase the ability of underserved communities to identify, redress, remediate, and create awareness and accountability around environmental concerns, her organization, Public Lab,[3] has empowered more than 50 local organizations and thousands of individuals around the United States and beyond, putting *possibilitivity* into practice.

Let's take an even more extreme example. Who would think it possible to empower women in rural, mountainous Pakistan, a region rife with fundamentalism, where someone could be killed for even suggesting change? Mission impossible, you say?

Well, Arif Khan[4] believed differently. His vision was to market traditional handicrafts produced by women in underserved Pakistani communities, bringing economic development to remote mountainous areas of the country. Working through thorny cultural issues, Arif has modernized Pakistan's handicraft industry, taking the women's products into the fashion mainstream as exclusive items. His organization, Mashal, provides women with the raw materials they need and then helps them market their products. The women receive business training and are encouraged to organize themselves into small groups of entrepreneurs and begin ventures of their own. With improved skills, sturdier products and an ability to market them effectively, rural women artisans are empowered to grow their mini-businesses and generate more income. Bringing money to their families raises their social status in the community, and additional resources promote better access to education and basic family health needs. Arif has indeed made the impossible happen.

Again, possibilitivity is not a matter of boldness, nor is it merely a matter of intelligence. Intelligence bolsters resolve and conviction, but many a bright skeptic has argued that a thing cannot be done. No, possibilitivity is embedded not in the IQ, but in a deep-seated drive to perceive the seemingly undoable as doable.

Similarly, we shouldn't confuse possibilitivity with self-efficacy. One might have great confidence in one's own abilities yet still perceive a challenge as undoable. Nor is it simply optimism. One can believe that good ultimately prevails over evil and still perceive a specific challenge as impossible to accomplish. No, possibilitivity would seem to be a distinct human quality that, when applied, produces extraordinary power.

---

[3] See https://publiclab.org/ (retrieved March 16, 2019).
[4] See www.ashoka.org/en/fellow/arif-khan#intro (retrieved March 16, 2019).

Working Wonders: How to Make the Impossible Happen

It's fair to say that what these individuals have achieved, in spite of obstacles and naysayers, is nothing short of magical – hence the phrase "Working Wonders" in the title of this book. But this "magic" isn't achieved by removing all constraints (consider the imprudence of that trek in the mountains in dangerous weather). Instead, the real magic comes when we're able to strike a balance between go-for-the-gold determination and close-minded complacency or fear.

Striking the Balance

Let's imagine that there are two basic forces pulling your mind in opposite directions. One defends the fortress of the mind against perceived threats such as change and risk. The other advocates for the mind's openness to opportunity and possibility. Interestingly, this happens with all living matter, starting with a primitive, single-celled paramecium. The floating organism has barriers to fend off unwanted particles and toxins but also a mechanism to absorb what is wanted and to adjust to the environment. Those two tendencies – to protect from what's unwanted and invite what's wanted – are kept in balance, allowing all living creatures to both maintain their integrity and interact with (and eventually adapt to) their environment.

The real blessing is that our minds naturally have a good balance between the two, and the harmony that exists between them can generate some surprising and positive results.

Opposition Through Humor in the Polish Underground Solidarity Movement

A good example of this dichotomy is the Polish underground movement, Solidarity, which during the 1980s, staged nonviolent opposition to the totalitarian communist regime. Tanks were in the streets, thousands of people had been arrested, the entire telephone network was switched off, mail was heavily censored, all broadcasting media were banned except for a few official propaganda sources, train travel was severely restricted and required special permission, and on the roads private cars were searched at frequent checkpoints.

Yet, with many of the movement's leaders imprisoned or in hiding, this decentralized effort became a powerful, widespread, and efficient operation involving as many as 10 million people.[5]

Through bottom-up initiatives, Solidarity activists set up a secret technical unit that regularly published and widely distributed illegally printed materials, without the availability of printing presses or chemical ingredients for making printing ink. They supported underground educational services. They held clandestine, illegal art exhibits and home-based theatrical performances with actors who were banned from, or who boycotted, the public stage. And they executed well-orchestrated national demonstrations of civil disobedience.

The challenge was to find a way to oppose while avoiding being arrested. On one hand, the mind's "protective" forces gave rational excuses to steer clear of danger: "Don't imperil your career." "Remember, you have a family to care for." "Why you? Let others take the risk." On the other, the mind's "open" forces created a drive to contribute to the Solidarity activity: "Someone has to stop those arrogant communists." "Risk taken now will contribute to a better future for our children." "It feels good to belong to this underground community and feel comradeship with others."

I participated in this movement and saw first-hand that a balance between those forces led to some smart and effective strategies. I was often struck by the way humor was used to find alternative and unexpected solutions. It sounds like an oxymoron, but rather than confront the system, we chose to ridicule it, using humor to thwart authority and build our own alternative civil society in spite of the tanks in the streets.

For example, in big cities, people effectively boycotted the government-sponsored TV news. Each evening, at exactly 7:30 p.m., when the government-sponsored broadcast began, people left their homes to take walks around their neighborhoods, socializing with other families along the way. This cheerful event lasted until 8:00 p.m. sharp, when the nightly news ended and everybody returned home for dinner. The police were helpless to stop this "protest," given that no one was verbally or physically confronting the regime. However, the collective action, taking place at a specific time, made a powerful impact and sent a strong, albeit *sub rosa*, message.

The movement also developed an uncanny ability to work with whatever was available, given that there were severe shortages, both unplanned

---

[5] See Kenney (2001, 2008); Ash (2002); Brown (2003); Osa (2003); Praszkier (2019).

and intentional. Members of the underground found a way to make printing ink by mixing cleaning agents and shoe polish and devised portable printing equipment that could fit into a backpack. Manuals on how to make the printing equipment were disseminated. Activists would meet, assemble the equipment, print their materials, pack up their presses, and disappear into the crowd. In this way thousands of small publishing units were tasked with the ongoing job of printing and distributing illegal newsletters, magazines, and banned books.

In one instance the secret police identified one of the backpackers and created a trap near the house where he was suspected of printing illegally. Local activists monitored the police radio dialogue with home-made receiving units and reacted with agility by sending a few dozen similarly dressed backpackers out to walk the nearby streets. This confused the police and allowed the real printing agent to escape.

Perhaps the best example of citizens finding a way to be engaged without endangering themselves was the Orange Alternative.[6] This citizen group staged more than 60 "happenings," using absurdity to attack the regime and send a strong message. One event cleverly addressed the chronic shortage of toilet paper. At Christmastime an activist dressed as Santa Claus stood in a main square, giving away toilet paper for free. A huge crowd gathered, waving their toilet paper and laughing about it. The police were helpless to act because no law was broken, even though the spectacle made them look ridiculous. When the police did step in and arrest the activist dressed as Santa, the crowd chanted, "Free Santa Claus!" Because he'd done nothing illegal, he was soon released. Afterward Santa Claus remained a symbol of resistance, and buildings were covered with drawings of his iconic cap, putting authorities in the embarrassing position of having to scrub walls all over town.[7]

These ingenious forms of protest came out of a desire to voice opposition without risking imprisonment, in other words a tug-of-war between protective and open forces. Keeping in mind that this balance creates the magic or Wonder that makes the impossible possible, in Part II we'll look at the mechanisms that work to keep the mind closed to possibility, and in Part III, we'll examine effective ways to open it up.

---

[6] Kenney (2001).

[7] See www.inyourpocket.com/wroclaw/Alternative-orange-movement_70296f and https://espionart .com/2017/02/24/ridiculing-the-regime-the-orange-alternative-in-poland/ (both retrieved March 16, 2019).

PART II

Entrenching and Defending the Fortress

If we think of the mind as a well-protected fortress, we can identify the various layers of reinforcement that stifle our possibilitivity (Figure 5). Let's take a closer look at each.

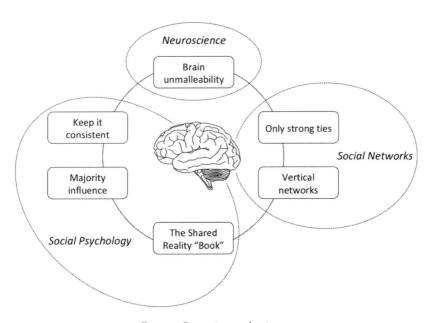

Figure 5 Protective mechanisms.

CHAPTER 5

Brain Unmalleability

It was when I experienced severe shoulder pain that I discovered the physical symptoms of harmful brain patterns. I consulted a few physical therapists who treated my rigidity with massage and stretching exercises, but their therapies didn't help. Finally I found one who used a holistic approach to help the body restore its natural balance. His treatment method was to use non-invasive manual techniques focused on inter-related and mutually influencing groups of muscles. We soon discovered that the pain was due to an unnatural position I took when standing or walking. The therapist recognized this posture as typical for easing pain in another part of the body. Asked if I had had some fall or accident in the past, I recalled that a few years earlier I had fallen down and badly hit the ribs on the other side of my body. The incident was very painful, and for some time afterward, I compensated by hunching over when I walked. My a-ha moment during my shoulder therapy came when I realized that my brain must have been storing this bizarre posture years after the original pain was gone and forgotten.

After that experience, I wanted to learn more about what causes us to cling to old patterns that can cause us to become as rigid and inelastic in how we think as how we move. And as I dug deeper I discovered an increasing interest in the phenomenon of brain plasticity as an area of study. In this case, the word plasticity means pliability and malleability. It's the capacity of neurons and neuronal connections in the brain to change in response to new experience.

Plasticity and Unmalleability

The brain's plasticity is fundamental to the adaptability of our behavior, learning and memory processes, brain development, and brain repair.[1]

---

[1] Sale et al. (2014).

Not surprisingly, plasticity is at its greatest during childhood. The toddler learns new movements, develops reactions to certain tones in his mother's voice and expressions on her face, etc. There's much to learn about a complex world. Simply grabbing a cup involves stretching and releasing dozens of muscles in the arms and fingers, coordinating movements to perform a harmonious action sequence aimed at achieving the desired result. First attempts are clumsy, but subsequent tries become more precise. And all of this is orchestrated by the brain, specifically by new neural pathways prompting new sets of operations.

The average human brain has about 100 billion neurons. Each neuron may be connected to more or less 10,000 other neurons, signaling to each other through more than 1,000 trillion synaptic connections.[2] Neurons activated to perform a certain function connect to each other to form neural networks. The connections between neurons change over time. The more signals sent between two neurons, the stronger the connection grows. With each new experience and each remembered event or fact, the brain slightly rewires its neural networks, stabilizing some pathways of connections and dissolving others.

The child repeating a movement, such as reaching for the cup, creates new connections, which become stable after several trials and, over time, turn into a pattern stored in its brain. At that point grabbing a cup, while still involving dozens of well-harmonized muscle operations, becomes a fully automated action requiring no conscious thought.

Our brains store many of these automated patterns, together with their associated neuronal pathways, keeping them handy for whenever they're needed. On the one hand this is a blessing. We don't have to relearn how to scratch every time we have an itch, how to recognize anger every time we see someone scowl, or how to drive a car every time we want to go somewhere. On the other hand, many of our patterns may have been stored in response to specific circumstances, say, for example, a fall. The body sustains injury and tightens the shoulder muscles to soothe and isolate the pain. The mind stores this response to a temporary situation, and over time it becomes the default. Months after the original pain is gone, the stored response is still at work, and tightened shoulder muscles cause secondary pain. The same thing can happen with automated reactions to people or words. If someone named Steve put you down in a hurtful way, you might have stored the neuronal pathways of your response, which reactivate whenever you meet someone with that name, even years later.

[2] Mastin (2018).

The good news is that many of those stored default neuronal pathways can be reversed through physical therapies and body techniques, such as the Feldenkrais approach (see Chapter 23), or through new positive experiences, such as getting to know a terrific Steve. The real problem, however, is that as we get older, the general tendency to form new neuronal pathways decreases. The brain tends to rely on existing connectivity patterns and, over time, become less malleable, making it more difficult to change our ways.

Perceiving New Challenges

This gradual decrease in malleability has a direct influence on how we perceive new challenges. The unfamiliar exists outside of stored patterns and thus automatically evokes an avoidance reaction. The toddler encountering an unknown situation immediately jumps in, be it opening a newly discovered drawer in grandpa's desk or a pot on the stove. The drive to explore the unknown and instigate new neural connections at that age is predominant. But after decades have passed, the same individual encountering a novel situation receives a powerful signal that says "don't get involved."

What has happened is that over time that former toddler has assembled enough stored patterns to be comfortably adapted to his environment, so there seems to be no need to "force" new neural connections. The brain's signal to avoid novel challenges becomes primal, and the mind subconsciously produces a rationale to support this reaction: "It's not doable." "Many have tried and failed." "Why me? Let others try."

We may perceive these reactions as cold-hearted and selfish. But their primal function is to lend a hand and provide a rationale after the brain automatically rejects the request for a new neural connection. Unmalleability becomes one of the custodians of the mind, defending the entrance to the fortress and "instinctually" classifying new challenges as unreachable.

Examples of "No Way" Reactions

The science behind the brain's plasticity is intriguing, but the real-world consequences of mental unmalleability are far less esoteric. Imagine that you're a teacher struggling with poor student achievement in inner cities. You think that one of the problems is that good teachers teach in these poor neighborhoods for a year or two, then burn out and quit. High turnover damages much-needed continuity in relationships with students, and the exodus of effective teachers leads to teacher shortages and effectively sentences a country's neediest children to low-quality education and a lifetime of fewer opportunities. You want to figure out how to retain really good teachers in disadvantaged communities, but when you bring it up with the powers that be, the negative reaction is immediate, and the rationale pops up instantly. The problem is deemed "unsolvable," and poor education persists.

Or let's say that you're concerned with the prevailing phenomenon of employees taking care of personal issues during work time. "Presenteeism," or non-productive presence at work, is becoming an increasingly common problem in organizations. People all over the world spend about 20 percent of their work time on personal business: searching the internet for vacation opportunities, arranging to pick up their children from school, finding a last-minute gift for a spouse's forgotten birthday, etc. Sometimes using an employer's time for personal stuff is unavoidable. However, it usually creates a problem for managers and derails harmony in the workplace.

It's a real issue. But suggest a creative solution and expect to get a negative reaction, followed by rational arguments along the lines of "it happens everywhere. Trying to change it is like nailing jelly to the wall."

Or suppose you're an individual with autism who has, as a result of your condition, unique insight into the feelings and perceptions of animals. You have big ideas about how to make the treatment of livestock more humane. But will anyone listen?

These real-life examples of the mind's unmalleability in the face of possibility demonstrate our propensity to reflexively say "no way."

We will later see how these three impossibility examples were turned into possibilities. On the other hand, the same assemblage of templates for the neural connections that tell us to steer clear of the "new" also create the foundation upon which wisdom is built. Without a phalanx of neural connectivity patterns fixed and fighting for stability, our lives would be rife with risk and turmoil. Our challenge is to strike a balance between the "stop" and "go," without falling into one of the extremes. And a good place to start is by looking at the ways in which our minds work to keep us safe.

CHAPTER 6

Keep It Consistent

Festinger's Concept of Cognitive Dissonance

When I was a teen I had an image of myself as clumsy, heavy, and bereft of athletic ability. My harsh self-assessment was confirmed every time I missed the ball – a failure extracted from reality and stored as evidence of my clumsiness. Firm in my belief that sports weren't my thing, I deleted from my awareness all the times when I made the play and seemed, in fact, a fairly agile fellow. It wasn't until I learned to swim and began to out-perform my colleagues in competition that I was forced to challenge my image of myself as a total klutz. But even as my negative self-image began to crumble, I struggled, hesitant to try volleyball, running, and other activities. Finally, compelled by a desire to try, e.g., jogging, which turned out to be very successful, I took a leap of faith and discovered that I was actually quite adroit and nimble. My self-image changed and I was then hungry to exercise, compete with colleagues, and try new games.

Years later, studying social sciences, I understood that I had been deadlocked with my negative (though consistent) self-image and any contradictory evidence was an unwelcome shock to the status quo. It was Leon Festinger's concept of cognitive dissonance that clearly explained what had happened to me.

We humans have a need to explain the world around us, both to our-selves and to other people. We do it constantly. Highly motivated to assign causes to our own behavior and that of others, we hang reasons on the events we see or hear about. In social psychology this tendency is called *attribution*. Not only do we try to explain everything, we also go to great lengths to keep all of our attributions, attitudes, and beliefs in harmony.[1] It was Festinger who, in the 1950s, proposed that we strive for internal

---

[1] Jaspars and Fincham (1983).

psychological consistency in order to function harmoniously in the real world.[2]

When our attributions about the world and ourselves are cohesive, it makes us feel good. However, when they clash, or a discrepancy arouses, it evokes a state of tension known as *cognitive dissonance*. The experience of dissonance is unpleasant, so we're motivated to eliminate it by any means and reclaim our lost harmony. In Festinger's words, we strive to *reduce the cognitive dissonance*.

We do this either by modifying parts of our cognition or by adding new elements to it. Another option is to actively avoid social situations or contradictory information that could increase the cognitive dissonance. Festinger uses the example of eating a doughnut while on a diet to demonstrate that people generally reduce their cognitive dissonance in four ways:[3]

- Some people justify the behavior by changing a "no doughnut at all" stance to "I'm allowed to cheat on my diet every once in a while."
- Others justify the behavior by adding a new element: "I'll spend thirty extra minutes at the gym to work off the doughnut."
- In some cases people simply ignore or deny information that conflicts with existing beliefs: "This doughnut doesn't contain a lot of sugar."
- Finally, it's possible to simply change the behavior or the cognition: "I'll eat no more doughnuts."

More light was shed on the methods used for reducing cognitive dissonance in longitudinal research from the International Tobacco Control (ITC). In the study,[4] in order to reduce cognitive dissonance, smokers adjusted their beliefs to correspond with their actions:

- Some developed "functional" beliefs supporting their dissonant actions, such as "smoking calms me down when I am stressed or upset," "smoking helps me concentrate better," "smoking is an important part of my life," or "smoking makes it easier for me to socialize."
- Others used risk-minimizing beliefs: "the medical evidence that smoking is harmful is exaggerated," "one has to die of something, so why not enjoy yourself and smoke," or "smoking is no more risky than many other things people do."

---

[2] Festinger (1957).
[3] Festinger et al. (2009).
[4] Fotuhi et al. (2013).

We all have it – this desire to shore up our thoughts and opinions. Take for example the decision to buy a car. Once we've made our choice, we tend to avoid positive information about other brands and ignore any criticism related to the brand we have chosen. We may even seek out positive accounts related to the car of our choice. These self-bamboozling methods nourish our cognitive consistency. We use them to protect our egos as well. Say we get a flat tire while driving. We might attribute this misfortune to a hole in the road (an external attribution), thereby preserving our self-image as a good driver. By assigning blame to external conditions, we avoid attributing the cause to our bad driving (an internal attribution), which would shatter the harmony of our self-concept.[5]

The fellow with a bias against Steves is another good example of Festinger's concept. Imagine that this person reinforces his prejudice by collecting stories supporting the conviction that Steves are malicious, and ignores all information to the contrary. Then at some point he has an unavoidable encounter with a Steve who is kind, supportive, warm, and caring. Now his cognitive harmony is upset and something has to be done to reduce the dissonance. Maybe he accepts this person as the exception that proves the rule to reestablish cohesion. Or perhaps he calms the waters by determining that the Steve, while a pleasure at work, must be a monster at home. Or, ideally, this fellow realizes his bias and takes on the challenge to root out his attributions against Steve and reorganize his cognitive structures so that he no longer perceives them as different.

These are simplistic examples of the power and prevalence of dissonance, but our desire to maintain cognitive harmony in the face of complex social issues can make progress difficult if not impossible. Let's go back to our "no way" examples mentioned in the previous chapter.

"No Way" Examples, Continued

Consider the challenge to improve the education system in inner cities. There exists a powerful, cohesive belief that inner cities are failed urban areas beyond repair, and inner-city schools provide primary evidence of the irreparable nature of the damage. Even researchers have argued that inner-city students aren't motivated (Miami University)[6] and that inner-city

---

[5] Bem (1967); Moskowitz (2005).
[6] Baker and Fultz (2010).

teachers, disillusioned by the discrepancy between what they thought their professional role would be and what it has become, must debate whether to educate kids or focus on keeping them off the streets (University of Delaware).[7] Opinions, experiences, and biases stack up to support the conviction that improving education in inner cities is mission impossible.

So what happens when the "believers" encounter a passionate individual committed to bringing change to education in disadvantaged urban areas? The ever-present drive to reduce cognitive dissonance typically kicks into high gear as they lay down a solid rationale: "Sounds nice, but this guy is a dreamer." Or, "She must be thinking about a very specific community already primed for improvement." Or, "He must have some big money behind him."

Or take the very real problem of "presenteeism." It's inevitable that employees will spend some amount of work time dealing with personal matters. This usually creates disharmony in the workplace. To forbid employees from dealing with personal stuff at work seems impractical, but to expect employers to tolerate lost productivity also seems unreasonable.[8] It would seem to be a problem without a solution. So when some "naïve" soul proposes to not only eliminate the problem, but also to turn it into a win-win situation, they run smack into an entrenched belief to the contrary and a reflexive urge to contradict and reduce the dissonance: "You can't generate revenue from someone searching online for a vacation spot." Or, "There's no real solution, so what you propose must be a trick."

And what about the notion of an autistic person "changing the world"?[9] The dominant view of autism is laden with prejudice. Parents of autistic children know the pain of other people's reactions all too well: "At that moment, you feel the stigma that societies around the globe attach to autism. In different ways and to different degrees, people in many countries view autism as a source of disappointment, annoyance, shame or worse."[10] This stigma led the Autism Research Institute to issue a Statement on Rights, Discrimination, and the Need for Social Change. And in 2015, United Nations' experts issued a document stating that discrimination against autistic people is the rule, rather than the exception.

Given the general public's cohesive bias, the best we might hope for is compassion: "Poor child, poor parents," we say and move on. But imagine

---

[7] Machik (2000).
[8] Krumrie (2014); Rosenberg McKay (2016).
[9] Citing the title of David Bornstein's book, *How to Change the World* (Bornstein, 2004).
[10] Sarris (2015); UN Rights Experts (2015).

meeting someone passionate about the potential of those with autism. This person tells you she's an autistic woman with a Ph.D., who achieved major social and environmental change in the United States and Canada, and your cognitive cohesion is shattered. You attempt to repair the damage, crafting some "reasonable" explanation for the anomaly: "She must not have been truly autistic." Or, "She must have had help – someone else doing most of the work." It's a natural response. We instinctively feel the need to counter any assault on the beliefs that help us make sense of the world. And yet these three "dreamers" persisted in shaping a new reality. We'll share the outcome of their stories in a bit. But for now, as you envision the fortress of the mind, consider this need for cohesion to be one of its most formidable gatekeepers.

CHAPTER 7

Majority Influence

Another natural but inherently limiting behavior is conforming to the majority view.[1] Most of us have experienced the soothing feeling of belonging and the reinforcement inherent in shared opinions. It's why we follow fashion trends, join political groups, form hobby clubs, or swear allegiance to one sports team over another.

I remember when I was a kid, my classmates and I believed that someone in the neighborhood was keeping a bear at home. We organized vigils to observe our neighbor walking his bear, left food for the bear on his front porch, and spent much of our time telling each other stories about the bear. Those of us in the know decided to keep it secret at school, though we couldn't resist leaking a few bear-related revelations. The other kids were in awe and treated us with the utmost respect, believing that we had actual contact with the bear. I remember how proud I felt being part of this bear conspiracy. Needless to say, after a few months the story, unsupported by evidence, fell apart. Nonetheless, the feeling of belonging endured.

The tendency to comply with the majority is called the *majority influence*. The fact is, we simply want to be liked, and sharing beliefs similar to those held by others increases the likelihood that we'll win approval and acceptance. Another basic need is the need to be right and logical; we want to believe that our judgments are correct and rational. Of course it's ideal when we're able to have both – when we believe that the opinion of the majority is also the correct one. As it happens, however, sometimes they're at odds.

The Asch Conformity Experiments

It was Solomon Asch who, in the 1950s, contributed greatly to our understanding of what happens when those two tendencies conflict.[2] To

---

[1] Haun et al. (2013).
[2] Asch (1956).

conduct his research he assembled groups of between seven and nine individuals in a classroom and told them they were participating in a simple experiment in visual distinction. At first glance the task seemed straightforward. There were four lines drawn on the board. One was called out as the standard, and the three others were of varying lengths. Two of the three were clearly equal in length to the standard line, and one other obviously differed. Participants were asked to indicate which of the three lines was equal in length to the standard line. In each group, the first respondent seemed to get it wrong, pointing to a line that was incorrect. Then, disturbingly, others in the group would make the same incorrect choice.

The catch was that all but one of the participants in each group were covert experimental assistants. The unwitting participant watched in astonishment as person after person picked the wrong answer, and in doing so began to doubt his own answer and, in most cases, ultimately went with the group. Torn between the need to belong and the need to be right, one subject after another went against their own better judgment in favor of the majority opinion.

This experiment was repeated many times with different groups and, in most cases (about 74 percent), the subjects finally chose the same wrong line, following what the others did. Seventy-four percent! That figure validates the strength of majority influence, but we can take some comfort in the fact that 26 percent stuck to their guns and chose the correct answer.

The Asch experiment revealed one more important correlation: Whenever even a single covert assistant pointed to the correct line, the subject felt confident in also choosing the correct line, even if the others picked the wrong one. So it would seem that having even one ally can empower an individual to choose what is correct over what is popular.

The iconic Asch experiment shows us how majority views have the power to shape our lives, in the clothes we wear, the foods we eat, or the way we express ourselves on social media. Sometimes we even adjust our behavior to conform to the majority in spite of our personal preferences or beliefs. However, having someone around who shares our view instantly endows our individual opinion, even if it goes against the mainstream.

Another powerful drive that compels us to move with the herd is the need for group identity, delineated by Abraham Maslow as one of the five basic human needs.[3]

---

[3] Maslow (1943).

The Need for Identity

It's quite common for people, especially those lacking self-confidence, to forge an identity through affiliation with a group. The risk, however, is that to belong, one must match one's own behavior to that of the group and subsume one's own identity into the group's identity. To paraphrase Descartes' "I think, therefore I am," in this case it becomes "I comply with the group, therefore I am." For people who feel lost, such belonging can boost self-esteem, especially if the group engages in healthy activities such as outdoor adventure, music, or advocacy. If, however, the group bolsters its own image by denigrating others, the positive self-image shaped from participation might be fleeting.[4]

Young people seeking to corroborate and affirm their identities are particularly inclined to join clubs, social media discussion groups, and other groups with well-defined rituals and adopt the group's way of thinking. This is part of the natural maturation process, and, in most cases, is a positive experience. However, depending on the circumstances, if, for example, he experiences family dysfunction or lacks basic security, a youngster's search for identity can lead him astray. Gangs, hate groups, and other destructive entities can offer vulnerable individuals a powerful, if misguided, self-identity. When the need to build and affirm one's identity overpowers other social norms and any identity is better than none, these highly structured groups can pose a tempting alternative.[5]

In most cases the process of confirming one's own identity doesn't lead to anti-social behavior, though it often includes compliance with the group's rituals, norms, stereotypes, and declared beliefs. As a result, an individual's own sense of possibilitivity often becomes constrained by the group.

A Double-Edged Sword

I am by no means suggesting that majority influence is always bad. Rather, it's a double-edged sword, sometimes shaping group thought for the better and sometimes for the worse. When the majority champions a healthy, non-smoking lifestyle and you go along with the trend, you benefit. When a community places particular value on empathy, it's good for everyone. But majority influence can also turn destructive, whether it leads to hunting witches in 1692 or driving the stock market off a cliff in the 1920s.[6]

[4] Cialdini and Goldstein (2004); McLeod (2007).
[5] Erikson (1993); Oswalt (2010).
[6] Grant (2013).

Doing the Impossible? No Way!

Business and social innovators by definition seek new solutions to pressing problems. If these problems are big enough to get their attention, it's likely that others have tried to tackle them before without success. These failures usually fortify the majority opinion that the problem is impossible to solve, compounding the innovators' challenge to address not only the problem but also the mindset that nothing can be done. Possibilitivity is besieged, as people become entrenched in a "no-way" response to new ideas.

That's why it takes special individuals to stand up to majority influence and overcome pervasive skepticism. Looking back at our three examples (improving the education system in inner cities, turning personal issues at work into a profitable activity, and fostering leadership in those with autism), it's easy to see why those seeking solutions ran headlong into vociferous naysaying, and why their ability to sustain possibilitivity in the face of such fierce resistance does look a bit like magic.

CHAPTER 8

Connections That Close the Mind

Small Worlds

While the desire for cohesiveness and like-mindedness can threaten our ability to think big, possibilitivity may also fall prey to the social networks we inhabit. Our first sphere of influence includes those we are closest to. Family members and close friends constitute close-knit circles of connection that stand the test of time and distance. Even if communication is sparse, just knowing that you're still connected to your old school buddies can sustain a feeling of closeness and support. This is our individual social capital, which supports our activities and, by its mere existence, increases our feelings of security and confidence to take risks.

In network theory, these close-knit circles are called *small worlds*. In the past, theorists thought that our global network was made up of a collection of these small worlds existing in isolation. That notion was then expanded to introduce the idea of weaker connections among the small worlds that served to bridge and expand our social capital.[1]

In the 1960s Mark Granovetter introduced the concept of strong and weak ties.[2] Strong ties were the connections inside each small world, while weak ties were those slender bonds between the distant circles. Concluding his research on how people get and sustain jobs, Granovetter coined the idea of the "power of weak ties." That is, it isn't the strong bonds that provide the greatest opportunities for employment, but the distant connections that are more likely to open doors to completely new opportunities. The global network came to be seen as myriad small worlds, most of which were inter-connected through weak ties. If a member of one small world is connected with a member of another small world, all the participants of both clusters would potentially be linked.

---

[1] Barabási (2003).
[2] He was conducting research on the subject of how people "network." See Granovetter (1973, 1983, 1995).

Ideally, we strike a balance between strong and weak ties.[3] Strong ties are relationships among people who work, live, or play together. They create a *bonding* type of social capital and provide a societal backbone. They help maintain and transmit values and traditions, provide a sense of identity, and serve as reference points in case of disturbances. Weak ties create a bridge between strong-tie networks, keeping us open to new connections and opportunities.

Having too many weak ties may make us feel baseless and cut off from our roots. Too few or no weak ties and we're trapped within a small circle of influence closed off to new ideas. People deprived of information from distant parts of the social system and confined to the provincial news and views of their close friends can find themselves bound by groupthink and at a competitive disadvantage in the marketplace of ideas. It also follows that a strong-tie dominant network would discourage possibilitivity and reinforce resistance to novel ideas coming from outside the close-knit circle.

Vertical Communication

Researchers conducting a longitudinal study looked at innovation within manufacturing firms and found that the most novel developments come from collaborative networks comprising different types of partners.[4] When we think about connections in the workplace, we envision vertical information flow, with guidance and control coming from the top, and reporting coming from the bottom. But a less traditional model employs the horizontal or lateral flow of information, across departmental boundaries or functional areas, at a given level of an organization; in other words, people at the same level communicate more freely.

Vertical communication enables upward or downward hierarchical influence. Upper-level management conveys suggestions, complaints and recommendations to subordinates and collects information from subordinates to inform decision-making. It's also useful for assigning jobs and evaluating performance.

But vertical communication has also several disadvantages. Downward communications can become distorted as they make their way through the multiple levels of an organization, or they can get hung up along the way, making it difficult for managers to convey information and

---

[3] Praszkier (2012); Joseph (2018).
[4] Nieto and Santamaría (2007).

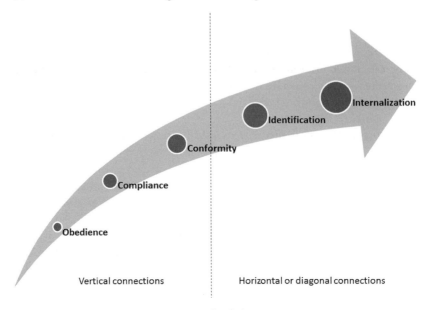

Figure 6 Levels of adaptation.

collect feedback. Worse, this structure can enable dependency and curb motivation. In my previous book, *Empowering Leadership of Tomorrow*,[5] I reviewed the multiple levels of adaptation (see Figure 6).

In the case of vertical communication, adaptation remains on the more superficial obedience-compliance-conformity level, whereas free horizontal communication is a gateway for a deeper identification with and internalization of the organization's objectives. There is heated discussion in the educational and business sectors on how compliance as an overarching management style stifles creativity.

The message, again, is about striking the right balance between vertical and horizontal communication. If vertical communication dominates, people can become overly reliant on those above them. Adopted as a personal style, it could lead one to look for similar direction in all aspects of life. Analogous to groupthink this may be seen as a "top-think" approach. And it can be equally detrimental to the fair evaluation of a new idea. Skepticism delivered from a place of authority can quash any sense of possibilitivity.

Not to say that vertically connected organizations can't achieve great things. Those who establish Corporate Social Responsibility (CSR) programs are great examples. Organizations that measure performance using the Triple Bottom Line (3BL) instill a top-down care for social, environmental, and economic issues. Others, like Google, have embraced slogans such as "Don't be evil." Some firms are embedding social goodness into their business. People Water,[6] through their "Drop for Drop" initiative, use sales of bottled water to help fund clean-water projects, such as well repair and water purification, in impoverished nations around the world. Done well, CSR programs can even be profitable. (See Paul Herman's book, *The HIP Investor*, in which HIP stands for "Human Impact + Profit.")[7]

CSR programs are often imposed and managed vertically, but they can also take shape as horizontal, employee-driven initiatives, such as volunteer programs.[8] In fact, some say the horizontal model is more efficient, because the top-down model disregards the security and fairness needs of employees who play a decisive role in accomplishing CSR.[9]

Finding the Balance

It's easy to see how people limited in their connectivity to small worlds (isolated close-knit circles) and vertical connections could react with virulent skepticism to, for example, the novel idea to reform inner-city schools, or to solve "presenteeism," or to change the world in spite of being autistic. On the other hand, someone with a healthy balance of strong and weak ties and multiple horizontal and diagonal connections to broaden their perspective might be more receptive.

[6] See www.peoplewater.com (retrieved March 16, 2019).
[7] Herman (2010).
[8] Bovee and Thill (2011).
[9] See, for example, Naccache et al. (2017).

CHAPTER 9

Personal Book on Shared Reality

So now we know some of the reasons why possibilitivity gets squelched: the neuronal connectivity patterns that allow us to learn decrease the brain's plasticity over time; we're driven by a need to explain the world and to attribute reasons to events and behaviors; we crave consistency and go to great lengths to reduce cognitive dissonance; we need to identify with something bigger than ourselves; and most of us are susceptible to the influence of the majority. All of these mechanisms are part of the mind's attempt to shape a satisfactory reality. Of course, this raises the interesting question: what is real?

How Real Is Real[1]

> The mind is organizing the world through organizing itself. (Jean Piaget – the famous Swiss father of the psychology of learning and child development)

> What we see changes what we know. What we know changes what we see. (Jean Piaget)

This motto suggests that reality as we perceive it is not *the* reality. Instead, our perceived reality changes along with our mind's perception. New cognitions shape our mind and, in return, the reshaped mind perceives a reshaped reality.

Piaget was the great pioneer of constructivism, otherwise known as the "theory of knowing," which says that we construct reality in the process of cognition. However, modern constructivists have added a social component, saying that it is not only our minds that shape our perceived realities, but also our social relations.

---

[1] Quoting the title of Paul Watzlawick's book, *How Real Is Real?* Watzlawick (1997).

This social take on constructivism became prominent in the United States with Peter Berger and Thomas Luckmann's 1960s book, *The Social Construction of Reality*. They argued that all knowledge, including the most basic and common-sense information, comes from and is sustained by social interactions. The theory of social construction (SC) says that our understanding of the world, including the meaning we give to encounters with others, is influenced by social context. SC also assumes that this construction of reality is done jointly, in coordination with others, rather than individually. The next question is, why?

Social Identity Theory

The answer is embedded in the social identity theory (mentioned in the previous chapter), which says that we are intrinsically motivated to achieve positive distinctiveness – a positive self-concept that we form and affirm through identification with a social construct.[2]

The twentieth-century German-born American developmental psychologist Erik Erikson, who developed the concept of the "identity crisis," posits that at some stage in a teenager's development the need for identification is so strong that, if family or community fail to satisfy it, the teen may seek to identify with whatever is available, including alternative or even criminal groups.

Given that it's such an essential part of who we are, it's not surprising that social identity theory gets a lot of attention in organizational development. Employers who understand that employees who self-identify with the organization are the most engaged may invest heavily in teambuilding activities designed to encourage that identification.[3]

Personal Book on Shared Reality

Basically, we shape our reality by wrestling with our own cognition and dissonance, and we build shared cognition with the groups to which we belong. It was Shaun Gallagher who, in 2009, coined the term "participatory sense-making,"[4] referring to the ways we build our understanding of the world by "enacting" with others. Think of it as building a *shared reality*.[5] Once acknowledged by others and shared in a continuing process

[2] Erikson (1993).
[3] Brewer and Gardner (1996).
[4] Gallagher (2009).
[5] Term coined in the mid-1990s by Curtis Hardin and E. Tory Higgins (Hardin & Higgins, 1996).

of social verification, experience is no longer subjective, but rather achieves the status of objective reality. The individual creates and maintains the experience of reality or meaning by sharing it with others in a process of social verification.

This means that a significant bulk of our concepts are constructed in compliance with our social group or community. We build our own explanation of reality, but only through constant verification with how things are understood by others. This brings us back to *constructivism* and to Peter Berger and Thomas Luckmann, whose term *social construction of reality* became iconic. They even claimed that the only reality we can know is socially constructed.[6]

The stronger our identification with the group, the more our thoughts unify with prevailing opinions. This gives us a greater sense of control but may be illusive and deceptive. We think we understand the world, but we've really just submitted to the group's thinking. This is especially problematic when the group is insular and biased against the outside world, making it difficult to introduce new ideas that counter prevailing beliefs.

A good metaphor for this reality-construction process is that we are writing and maintaining in our mind a Personal Book of Shared Reality (let's call it the "Book"), which explains the world and the behavior of others. We compare our Book with others, add new chapters when new events or people appear, compare it with previously stored beliefs (through reduction of Festinger's dissonance), highlight certain excerpts when confronting certain people, etc. We continuously verify and confirm our Book with the group, adjusting as needed to maintain its consistency, even if new and unexpected information surpasses or contradicts its narrative.

The benefit of having the Book is that we're able to understand, classify, and judge external objects and events quickly, making it easier to comply with the group we identify with. The downside is that the Book often takes control of our cognition, limiting our space to doubt, explore, and struggle with challenging phenomena. If the prevailing conviction of your group is "no way," the Book can keep you from trying to tackle intractable problems, from proposing innovations that don't fit the mainstream, and from becoming passionate about new ideas.

Turning back to our three examples, the Book usually complies with the prevailing skepticism, especially when we encounter enthusiastic people who want to rock the boat, i.e., improve the education in disadvantaged urban areas (when "everybody knows" it's impossible), abate the conflict

---

[6] Berger and Luckmann (1967); see also Leeds-Hurwitz (2009).

between managers and employees who are using working time for their personal problems (obviously undoable), and change attitudes toward autistic people (ridiculous and unrealistic).

The Personal Book of Shared Reality is a powerful document capable of severely limiting our perception of what's possible. But as we'll see in a bit, with some preconditions, it can also convincingly play the role of a mind-opener!

Cognitive Bias

On the one hand, shared reality gives us comfort and confidence, but it can also get us into trouble when cognitive bias comes into play. Cognitive bias is the subjective and individual construction of a social reality that may cause us to form inaccurate judgments or illogical interpretations in business or personal life.[7]

In business, for example, one study showed that subjective judgments by planners and managers are a major component in the process of strategic planning.[8] If such judgments are being driven by faulty cognitive bias, their efforts are likely to be counter-productive.

Cognitive bias can also influence our family life. Take, for example, parents who worry about their child catching a cold. They over-dress him up to keep him warm, but now the kid is sweating, which actually causes him to catch a cold. The parents validate their excessive concern through their own actions, making it unlikely that they'll ever challenge their erroneous assumption that their child is particularly vulnerable to catching a cold.

From these examples and many others, it's easy to see that cognitive bias can be another stalwart defender determined to protect the fortress of the mind.

From Un-possibilitivity to Possibilitivity

By now, we've identified several culprits in the persistent and pervasive campaign to keep the mind closed to new ideas and resistant to the notion that we can overcome daunting challenges to achieve seemingly impossible things. It wouldn't surprise me if, at this point, you were feeling a bit hopeless in the face of the fierce opposition to innovation going on in

---

[7] Barnes (1984).
[8] Albert et al. (2000).

our own mind. But don't despair; just as our heroes Ricardo Semler, Mary Gordon, and Piotr Pawłowski displayed enduring possibilitivity despite unrelenting skepticism and doubt, we each have the capability to do the same. The next chapters will show you how to counter the forces of "unpossibilitivity" and unleash your ability to achieve amazing things.

PART III

Opening the Mind
Possibilitivity

Welcome back to the "it's doable" universe. In this part, as we leave behind the world of "no way," we'll take a look at the accomplishments of a few more inspiring change-makers and discuss a variety of mind-opening mechanisms found in the creative, scientific, and social realms and beyond (see Figure 7).

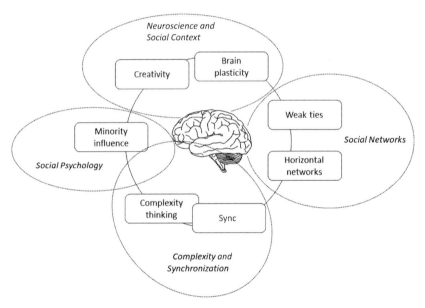

Figure 7 Mechanisms contributing to the enhancement of possibilitivity.

CHAPTER 10

They Did It!

Let's get back to those three stories introduced earlier and find out how the education system in a disadvantaged urban area could attract and retain the best teachers, how dealing with personal issues at work became a win-win situation for employees and employers, and how an individual with autism revolutionized the way the livestock is handled.

The Best Education in the Poorest Areas

As characterized in heart-wrenching films such as *Lean On Me*, *Dangerous Minds*, and *One Eight Seven*, too many inner-city kids struggle to get an education and too many inner-city teachers must choose between teaching their kids and keeping them safe and off the streets. A young university graduate, Temp Keller, knew it was a tough problem, but he was passionate about trying to make things better for these students and educators. So after graduating, he chose to work as a teacher in a low-income area of East Palo Alto. He was startled to see how quickly the best teachers in such schools – often graduates of the best universities who had chosen to work in low-income areas – became the first to burn out and quit. Indeed, research shows that teacher turnover is significantly higher in economically disadvantaged areas. And after five years three-quarters of the teachers in Keller's district had left.

This high turnover[1] disrupts not only the instructional flow but also the relationship between students and their teachers. Student self-esteem suffers when teachers – people they deem important – don't find it worthwhile to stay with them. Seeing the extreme needs of his students and the ways in which the system was failing them, Keller dedicated himself to finding a solution.

---

[1] For teacher turnover see Ingersoll (2001).

He realized that any lasting solution would have to include attracting and retaining the best teachers. To solve this problem, he founded Resources for Indispensable Schools and Educators (RISE)[2] to address the issue of attrition and to support teachers committed to improving student achievement. Attracting the best teachers to work in such schools was the first step, but the most critical challenge was keeping them. Keller's strategy through RISE included identifying teachers with commitment and then pre-screening schools to determine their level of support for teachers and willingness to include them in decision-making.

Keller also sought to ease the strain on committed teachers who used their own money to purchase classroom supplies, so he created RISE Rewards, certificates teachers can redeem for a wide range of classroom materials. RISE Rewards uses the online retail and delivery infrastructure created by the citizen group Adopt-a-Classroom. And only RISE teachers who remain with their school are eligible for the rewards, which creates additional incentive to stay on the job.

A third aspect of the RISE strategy is a strong teacher network designed to help innovative teachers share ideas and resources and give them the social and intellectual support they need to avoid burnout and remain committed to their low-income students.[3]

Keller's ideas worked. In disadvantaged neighborhoods, RISE teachers work in the best schools, receive needed financial support and remain active in the national teachers' network. Wearing their RISE badges with pride these teachers, who once struggled to earn respect, now enjoy high regard in their communities, signaling a significant mind shift. In the urban areas where they operate, they've remained durably committed, significantly lowering the turnover rate and raising the quality of education.

Restless in his success, Keller continues to devise creative ways to improve education. As a co-founding President of the Blyth-Templeton Academy,[4] he transforms the lives of students by providing highly individualized, experiential education in small classes with dedicated and skilled educators. As founder of WonderLab Learning,[5] he fosters children's curiosity, helps them develop skills in alignment with their passions, and

[2] See www.ashoka.org/en/fellow/temp-keller#intro; also www.idealist.org/en/nonprofit/a133f90d77 42408c8c6901103e88b059-rise-resources-for-indispensable-schools-and-educators-san-francisco (both retrieved March 16, 2019).

[3] This program began even before the incorporation of RISE: starting in 2000, Temp worked under the name of the CharterTeach Organization to award teaching fellowships.

[4] See www.blythtempleton.org (retrieved March 16, 2019).

[5] See www.wonderlablearning.com (retrieved March 16, 2019).

encourages them to be lifelong learners. Keller's remarkable achievements took dedication and hard work, but by removing the notion of "undoable" from the equation, he was able to solve intractable problems and make a huge difference in the lives of teachers, students, and their families.

Please Take Care of Your Personal Issues During Work Time!

As we know, and as HR specialists tell us, harmony in the workplace can provide excellent opportunity for personal development.[6] On the other hand, conflict between employees and employers can shatter trust, loyalty, and satisfaction, and stunt professional growth. And one of the most prevalent and intractable phenomena upsetting workplace harmony is the practice of taking care of personal issues during work time. Running errands, making travel plans, managing the family schedule, and countless other distractions can all cut into the workday.

"Presenteeism," as it's known, consumes about 20 percent of people's work time and, overall, costs businesses 10 times more than absenteeism.[7] It's an irritation for managers concerned about employee productivity and engagement and a point of contention for employees who feel undervalued and disrespected if they don't have enough autonomy to take care of a personal matter if they need to. It's a sticky problem, but that didn't keep Lucie Chagnon from finding a solution. Chagnon had been involved in community service in Montreal since the age of 17 when she developed a program to provide after-school activities to children from poor neighborhoods. She also founded a housing cooperative, a childcare center, and a women's center, as well as a business-consulting venture. Through her work she came to understand the potential for conflict around the issue of work–life balance. If "presenteeism" is inevitable, maybe we can at least derive some benefit from it, she thought.

The first step was to survey workers and identify the variety of personal issues being addressed during work time. Next, Lucy Chagnon contracted with small local organizations that could take care of these issues. Her solution was to provide a user-friendly platform through which employees could quickly access high-quality solutions to their problems. Employees exchange points that their employers provide for a comprehensive range of services including everything from daycare to transportation to pet-sitting

---

[6] See, for example, HCareers at www.hcareers.co.uk/article/employer-articles/achieving-harmony-in-the-workplace (retrieved March 16, 2019).

[7] Smith (2016).

Figure 8 One of the Commodus slides.
Received from Lucie Chagnon, the founder of Commodus.

to therapy. The platform, called Commodus ("accommodate" in Latin), provides services at the click of a button to save employees time at work, and employers who offer the services are viewed by their workers as caring, considerate, and respectful. Employees spend less time on personal matters and are more motivated, and the work environment is friendlier (see Figure 8).[8]

The program has been wildly successful and, to encourage rapid expansion, Chagnon created a franchise model that is available all over Quebec. Franchises have access to an online trade platform, and services are continuously monitored for quality and use and augmented as needed.

An additional advantage is that the tapestry of service providers, mainly public organizations, has grown stronger and more sustainable with the additional business. So really, it's a win-win-win: Employees gain an efficient high-standard platform for solving their problems (in many cases

---

[8] Figure 8 shows a slide designated for training employees; the project was implemented in the francophone areas of Canada.

purchasing additional points to use Commodus at home), companies receive better results and higher profit (as the employees are more loyal and committed), and service providers become more economically viable. Chagnon looked at the struggle to maintain work–life balance and devised an elegant solution using common sense, market principles, and human goodness. As a result, Commodus continues to attract attention and grow, to the benefit of many.

Autistic Woman Pioneers Humane Solution to Handling Livestock

Temple Grandin was born autistic in the mid-1940s, a time when autism wasn't well recognized and most autistic children were either diagnosed as "retarded" or simply institutionalized. It wasn't until the 1960s that our understanding and treatment of autism significantly changed.[9] However, Grandin's mother, Eustacia, was committed to her daughter's future and had the wisdom to go against the mainstream and give Grandin all the love and care she needed. She resisted specialists' recommendations to put her in a nursing home, and gave her daughter the kind of attention and training that was essential for her development and normal education.

It soon became apparent that Grandin had an extraordinary sensitivity, characteristic of many autistic persons. However, hers was to the feelings of animals. As a young teenager, Grandin spent time at a ranch where she developed a closeness with the cattle. She experimented putting herself in the place of the animals, physically crawling through animal chutes and experiencing first-hand what it felt like to be a cow. She recognized similarities in the ways that she and the animals experienced the environment and understood that animal-handling facilities were terrifying places for the cattle.

Grandin's autism induced a special relationship with animals in part because she sees in pictures – understanding the world more through vivid images than language. She also feels a heightened sense of fear, typical for autistic people, which causes hypersensitivity connected with an intense "fight or flight" instinct that can lead to intense panic.[10] Animals experience a similar "fight or flight" reaction in response to certain stimuli.

Grandin's ability to "see and feel" the way an animal does led her to look at the stressful way animals going to slaughter were handled. She looked

[9] Evans (2013, 2014).
[10] Scientists indicate that an enlarged amygdala (which Temple Grandin has) is the part of the brain that is responsible for anxiety and fear.

Figure 9 Temple Grandin with cattle.
Permission received from Temple Grandin.

at each animal's handling facility by visualizing it from the animal's stand-
point and identifying sounds, sights, or smells that might cause them to
be fearful and balk (see Figure 9).[11] Her hypersensitivity to sensory inputs
and sudden sensory changes gave her insight into the minds of cattle and
taught her to value the details to which animals are particularly sensitive, and to use her visualization skills to design thoughtful and humane
animal-handling equipment. She designed curving, serpentine walkways
that both prevent cows from seeing the slaughter up ahead and panicking
and give them the sensation that they are coming back around the same
way they came in. These solutions are spread across North America and
have become foundational in humane animal treatment around the world.

A Colorado State University colleague recalls a particular example of
Grandin's skill at a ranch where the handlers were having trouble moving
cattle through the serpentine chutes of Grandin's design.[12] Each time cattle
approached a particular part of the chute, the leader stopped, causing a
massive backup. Grandin watched what was happening and, with her
unique perspective, realized that the cattle were balking because sunlight

---

[11] Photo from Temple Grandin's office.
[12] See https://source.colostate.edu/temple-grandin/ (retrieved March 16, 2019).

was pouring through a hole in the chute. She recommended simply covering the hole with a piece of cardboard, a modification that instantly made the cattle smoothly move through the chute.

Grandin's work also benefitted those living with autism. While assuming the animal's perspective and crawling through narrow chutes, she noticed that mild physical pressure had a relaxing effect on her nerves. This observation led her to invent the "squeeze machine." Many people with autism are uncomfortable with physical contact such as hugging, handshakes, pats on the back, etc. Yet the relief Grandin felt when the chute in effect "held" her prompted her to devise a therapeutic, stress-relieving device she could crawl into and activate to feel its gentle pressure. Versions of her device are in use around the world to help calm hypersensitive people.

Grandin earned her Ph.D. and is currently a Professor of Animal Science at Colorado State University. Recognized as a global expert on the humane handling of animals, she is the author of several books, including *Thinking in Pictures: My Life with Autism*[13] and *Animals in Translation: Using the Mysteries of Autism to Decode Animal Behavior*.[14] Her books on autism[15] have become a popular resource for understanding how characteristics of autism, perceived by some as limitations, can be transformed into benefits. In the case of Grandin herself, her autism became a fulcrum for introducing global transformation in humane animal treatment.

It's not hard to imagine the level of skepticism these three individuals faced as they pursued their passions. Nonetheless, they persisted and had remarkable success. By now we have a pretty clear understanding of the naysayers' motivations. Now, let's look at the mechanisms that make us believe something is in fact "doable."

[13] Grandin (2006b).
[14] Grandin (2006a).
[15] See Temple Grandin's website for further information on her books: www.templegrandin.com/templegrandinbooks.html.

CHAPTER II

Brain Plasticity

For decades, the prevailing belief in neuroscience was that the adult human brain is essentially unchangeable and fixed, both in its structure and function. Fortunately, contemporary studies contradict this dogma and support the view that the human brain is much more plastic than previously believed, even as we age.

Brain plasticity is the capacity of neurons and neural connections in the brain to change in response to new experiences. Plasticity comes from the Greek word *plastos* meaning "formable." Brain plasticity (or neuroplasticity) refers to the extraordinary ability of the brain to modify its own structure and adapt to internal or external changes. This is a lifelong property of many species, especially humans. And it means that the brain has a fundamental ability to rewire itself to a certain extent.

My first experience with expanding the brain's plasticity came through the Feldenkrais Method. This technique, which we'll explore in more depth later, uses gentle, mindful movements to indirectly address the practitioner's physical problem and bring new awareness and possibility into all aspects of life. I discovered that one doesn't need to engage in painful stretching of muscles to move beyond a limitation. Instead, easy sets of gentle, painless, untypical movements can stimulate the brain to accommodate new experience.

For example, hard stretching targets the muscles and joints, which can be damaging in the long run. But playing and experimenting with small, intentional movements the brain doesn't expect can stimulate new neural connections and produce a novel experience. Even merely imagining movement may be enough to stimulate the brain's malleability, and thus enhance one's ability, in cases where physical exercise is too painful.

The Feldenkrais Method asserts that our limits exist not within our muscles and joints or our environment, but in our minds and the templates or patterns we've established throughout life. Some of those templates, stored when we experienced acute pain, remain long after the triggering event, limiting our capabilities. Replacing them with new templates makes the brain more flexible, and, as I experienced while following the Feldenkrais Method, improves both mental and physical flexibility, and in that way life!

Since that experience I've been fascinated with the brain's malleability. In my search for information, I've found contemporary studies that provide further evidence that the brain can change itself. For example, it's been documented that London taxi drivers tend to have a posterior region of the hippocampus that's larger than the same area of the brain in London bus drivers and non-professional drivers.[1] This part of the hippocampus specializes in acquiring and using complex spatial information in order to navigate efficiently. Because taxi drivers continually search for new routes, their brains change with their experience, provided the experience is long term.

In another study subjects who had lost their ability to see colors due to disease or injury took part in an experiment that used a device to transform colors into sounds.[2] After using this device continuously for eight years, the subjects had marked changes in neural patterns, structural connectivity and cortical topography at the visual and auditory cortex, compared with a control population. The subjects' brains literally changed in order to adapt to new information.

Brain malleability was also observed in the brains of bilingual people, namely in the left inferior parietal cortex, which is larger in those who are bilingual than in monolinguals.[3] In musicians who practiced at least one hour per day, researchers found that in several areas of the cortex – areas involved with playing music – gray matter volume was higher than in amateur musicians or non-musicians, indicating that the repeated act of playing music changes the brain's makeup and function.[4]

Brain malleability also plays a critical role in a variety of therapeutic programs used to treat brain injury, ADHD, and other problems.[5] Sets of brain exercises known as "brain training" help the brain adjust and change in order to overcome dysfunction[6] (more on this in the next section).

---

[1] Maguire et al. (2000, 2006).
[2] Alfaro et al. (2015).
[3] Mechelli et al. (2004).
[4] Gaser and Schlaug (2003).
[5] Dennison (1989); Johansson (2004); Doidge (2007).
[6] Draganski et al. (2006); Green and Bavelier (2008); Trayford (2014).

And brain plasticity most likely contributes to *cognitive flexibility*, which is the mental ability to switch between thinking about two different concepts, and to think about multiple concepts simultaneously (with the substantial role of hippocampus).[7] Doesn't it resemble divergent thinking?

All these examples, and many more, confirm that our brains are plastic! We now know that the brain is malleable not only in childhood, but also throughout adulthood and, most surprising, into old age, which is very good news for seniors.[8] Experience and learning, as well as development, can shape brain physiology, through connectivity and brain anatomy, and actually generate new brain cells. These changes may in effect be permanent. Enduring and stable, they last well beyond initial exposure to the learning experience.[9]

Pathways for the Brain to Rewire Itself

Let's take a closer look at some of the pathways that support brain plasticity. The most well-known is *synaptic brain plasticity*, which entails the development of new neuronal connections. This is especially dynamic at the beginning of life, when the brain accommodates new experiences and organizes itself accordingly. We mentioned before the example of a toddler learning to lift a cup, and how so many different muscles must be coordinated to execute this one movement. First trials are clumsy, until the brain sets up new neuronal connections, coordinating multiple sub-movements into one unified attempt. These new connections, repeated over time, become templates. This happens with all the new experiences, as the infant tries and experiments with new things. The brain is totally malleable, ready to absorb each new experience and set new neural connections.

Synaptic brain plasticity also occurs throughout adulthood, whenever something new is learned and memorized.[10] Even when we've stopped "growing," all new things we encounter and learn leave their mark by way of new neuronal connections. For example, studies have shown that intensive learning of abstract information can trigger plastic changes in the brain. Researchers examined the brains of medical students three months before their medical exams and right after and compared them to the

---

[7] Scott (1962); Rubin et al. (2014).
[8] Kramer et al. (2004); Jäncke (2009); Gu et al. (2013).
[9] Julie et al. (2004); Michelon (2008).
[10] Gerrow and Triller (2010).

brains of students who were not studying for the exams. The studying medical students' brains showed learning-induced changes in the posterior hippocampus and in regions of the parietal cortex, regions associated with memory retrieval and learning.

So we know that synaptic brain plasticity occurs throughout life, but are these changes lasting? How durable are those new neural pathways? Intuitively we might say, "use it or lose it." And that's exactly what's reflected in the studies: one new experience, even if remarkable, doesn't typically leave long-term neuronal connections, unless it's repeated and referred to several times. Fortunately, the neuronal connections that develop from repeated experience can form regardless of age. And because people now live longer and tend to remain healthier as they age, the potential for stimulating new neuronal connections is even greater![11]

Another plasticity pathway is *functional compensatory plasticity*, which happens when parts of the brain take over for other parts that aren't functioning properly. For example, in cases of brain injury or stroke, when some functions are limited, rehabilitation can awaken compensational mechanisms in which other parts of the brain can perform and support the disordered or even lost functions. New neuronal connections are established to replace the broken ones. As a result, some rehab programs aim to do much more than simply restore physical function, such as straightening a leg. They are more holistic and work to stimulate the brain's propensity for generating new neural paths.

An example of this is a program for educators working with children impaired with dysgraphia (the inability to write coherently due to brain disease or damage). In Dennison's Therapy, as it's known, children chart "lazy 8s" (the infinity symbol) in the air or draw symmetric figures with both hands (the Double Doodle technique). These techniques aren't aimed directly at writing per se, but they enhance brain plasticity, which, in turn, helps improve writing abilities.

Using these pathways the brain modifies itself by building new neural connections. But in another recently discovered form of brain plasticity called *neurogenesis plasticity*, new stem cells reproduce fully functioning brain cells. Our brains can actually produce new neurons! Let's dig a bit deeper into how synaptic and neurogenesis brain plasticity actually work and how they support our new ideas, especially those which surpass the customary limits of possibility.

---

[11] Kramer et al. (2004); Green and Bavelier (2008); Shelton (2013).

Synaptic Brain Plasticity

Neurons connect with other neurons through junctions known as synapses, and make possible everything we do in our lives. Given that the brain has about a hundred billion neurons, that network of connectivity is at a scale virtually impossible to grasp. Undaunted, a group of scientists launched the Human Connectome Project to attempt to describe the complete set of neural connections in the human brain.[12] While the network of anatomical connections linking the neuronal elements of the human brain is still largely unknown, scientists from many universities are now working to fill this gap. The new emerging science, known as *connectomics*, is replacing the previously predominant approach of identifying localized functions in the brain, as research indicates that the brain's functions are more closely tied to the connectome than to physical locations.

The brain's propensity for establishing new neuronal connections determines its plasticity or rigidity. Those connections are established directly, through synapses, but distant neurons may also communicate through chemical neurotransmitters such as serotonin, epinephrine (also known as adrenaline), norepinephrine (noradrenaline), endorphins, and dopamine that diffuse between the neurons of the brain.[13] These neurotransmitters also play a critical role in other aspects of life: dopamine helps control the brain's reward and pleasure centers, and endorphins are endogenous opioid peptides that provide pleasure and euphoria, something we'll explore further in Chapter 12.

Neurogenesis Brain Plasticity

The process of forming new brain cells is called *neurogenesis*, and as we've said, contrary to what was previously believed, this process continues throughout our lives. New neurons are born in several areas of our brains. This is good news for all of us, as we get older and fear mental decline. The bad news is that these new neurons generally die, unless our minds are active to solidify the pathway for the newly acquired experience or knowledge. Survival of these new neurons in the adult also depends on their ability to make functional contacts with existing neurons. Typically, about half of new neurons fail to integrate into existing neural networks and, as a consequence, die out.[14]

---

[12] Sporns et al. (2005); Sporns (2016).
[13] Shelton (2013).
[14] Klemm (2008).

So far, it's been documented that new neurons appear in the hippocampus, and around the hollow ventricles near the center of the brain.[15] Humans (and other mammals) have two hippocampuses, one on each side of the brain, and neurogenesis in this region plays an essential role in the consolidation of information from short-term memory to long-term memory, and especially in spatial memory that enables navigation; remember those London taxi drivers?

The adult brain continuously generates cohorts of neurons, and most newborn neurons integrate into existing neural circuits, demonstrating a unique cellular and synaptic flexibility in the adult brain. Current evidence indicates that the lifelong addition of new neurons may extend the child's early developmental plasticity to adulthood, which continuously refreshes the adult brain.

Brain Plasticity and Possibilitivity

It is probably brain plasticity that allowed Temp Keller, Lucie Chagnon, and Temple Grandin (our case studies from Chapter 10) to find novel and unusual solutions to solve pressing, yet insurmountable and protracted, problems. Navigating through the prevailing skepticism and finding ways to overcome obstacles and turn adversities into solutions required an avalanche of new neuronal connections, metaphorically speaking. It would be fascinating to study the hippocampal areas of their brains to see if they differ from a representative sample of society. My hunch is that in each case the hippocampus would be significantly larger than average, indicating expansive neuronal connectivity.

Brain plasticity is often viewed within the context of a single occurrence, such as a blind person learning to hear colors. My claim is that it can also be seen as a trait – an individual propensity for the brain to be plastic or flexible or, on the other extreme, to be nonmalleable (and a full spectrum of options in between). This tendency or trait is a key driver in our lives, as some people come to trust and rely on their brain plasticity, especially when facing challenges. "Naturally" seeing things as doable, even if they're commonly perceived as undoable, paves the way for higher possibilitivity, the conviction that turning the impossible into possible is within their reach.

---

[15] See, for example, Morrens et al. (2012).

CHAPTER 12

Creativity Opens Closed Doors

> Lost in Antarctica or confined to a prison cell, some individuals succeed in transforming their harrowing conditions into a manageable and even enjoyable struggle, whereas most others would succumb to the ordeal. (Mihály Csíkszentmihályi)[1]

> When creative people were asked to choose from a list the best description of how they feel when doing whatever they enjoy doing most – reading, climbing mountains, playing chess, whatever – the answer most frequently chosen was "designing or discovering something new ... it seems perfectly reasonable that ... some people ... enjoy discovering and creating above all else." (Mihály Csíkszentmihályi)[2]

Once, when I was in Africa, someone told me a story about a physics teacher in a remote, underserved area, who was concerned that his students were not interested in the subject. He was also sensitive to environmental issues, noting that the area was littered with soda cans. And he had a particular interest in figuring out how to provide hot water in areas that weren't on the electrical grid. After puzzling over these unrelated concerns, he came up with a creative solution to all three.

He organized a well-publicized competition, in which the local youth would first collect as many soda cans as possible and then hammer and polish them to create concave mirrors. The mirror configurations most effective at heating a bowl of water won the competition, and the students' families used them as a renewable energy source for heating water in pots and kettles.

The result was three-pronged: First, the students removed the litter, gaining some environmental education along the way; second, they learned how to use the concave mirrors to focus the sun's energy on one

---

[1] Csíkszentmihályi (1991, p. 90).
[2] Csíkszentmihályi (1997a, p. 108).

point, heightening their interest in physics through practical application; and third, local families received free access to hot water.

The teacher successfully merged three unrelated concepts – pollution, physics education, and off-grid energy – to achieve inspired solutions in a process known as "divergent thinking," a manifestation of creativity.

Are All People Creative?

Post-mortem analysis of the brains of some exceptionally creative people, such as Albert Einstein and Carl F. Gauss, revealed a marked expansion of the inferior parietal region, the area of the brain that is especially concerned with language and mathematical operations.[3] This proves that creative thinking and associated plasticity physically alters the brain. Put another way, a consequence of brain-changing plasticity is creativity.

While Albert Einstein is a classic example of this phenomenon, contemporary creative thinkers also abound. Take Elon Musk,[4] for example, who shaped his vision as CEO and CTO of SpaceX, CEO and chief product architect of Tesla Motors, chairman of SolarCity, and co-founder of PayPal. As an entrepreneur, inventor, and innovator, Musk personally participates in designing his electric cars and spaceships. He's committed to spreading the idea of renewable energy in housing, and he's involved in developing a high-speed transportation system known as Hyperloop. And Musk is in good company. Each year Fast Company selects the top 100 leaders shaping business in creative ways. Here's a handful of examples from the 2016 list:[5]

Amit Agarwal, from Bangalore, India, has introduced several innovations, including Amazon mobile photo studios that enable local businesses in smaller Indian cities to be active on the platform in less than an hour. He also launched over 3,500 neighborhood Amazon delivery and pickup points in stores and bakeries around India, increasing access to Amazon and bringing more clients into local businesses.

Karin Strauss, from Redmond, WA (a São Paulo native) is looking at ways to address the need for more data storage (projected to hit 16 zettabytes in 2017, the equivalent of 4 trillion DVDs). She, together with her colleagues at Microsoft Research and the University of Washington, are demonstrating that DNA storage technology could be the solution.

[3] Otte (2001).
[4] See https://astrumpeople.com/elon-musk-biography/ (retrieved March 16, 2019).
[5] See www.fastcompany.com/most-creative-people/2016 (retrieved March 16, 2019).

Information-dense and durable, DNA is also exceptionally resilient and recoverable. In April 2016, Strauss and her group of computer scientists and molecular biologists captured imaginations when they displayed a novel DNA data storage system.

Carlos Mario Rodriguez from San José, Costa Rica, successfully cross-bred Starbucks' first-ever hybrid to produce a high-yielding coffee plant that is also rust resistant. This is especially critical when coffee crops throughout South America buckle under leaf rust, a fungus that renders the plant unable to grow mature beans. Rodriguez introduced solutions that saved the plants from the fungus, and thanks to his innovation, Starbucks is giving away the superior seedlings to local biodiversity organizations.

Anna Young, from Cambridge, MA, co-founded Pop Up Labs, a company that runs the MakerNurse network to help frontline caregivers devise their own ways to improve medical care. She created stand-alone kits filled with supplies such as pliers, 3-D printers, laser cutters, and medical proto-typing equipment, which she sells to hospitals to encourage innovation. Using tools from Young's equipment, one nurse developed a new way to use bandages to dress the wounds of babies born with abdominal-wall defects, saving the hospital $250,000 in its first year of use. Young has also co-developed post-eye-surgery recovery kits and a solar-powered device for sterilizing medical instruments.

Brian Bannon, from Chicago, IL, believes that it's vital to reimagine the library as a place for experimentation and for democratizing both learning and technology. He is committed to transforming library learning tools, making them easily accessible to users of all ages. Along these lines, he has introduced a new library concept that includes Wi-Fi hot spots, robotics, and tablet computers – all that's needed to put contemporary technology in the hands of families that couldn't otherwise afford it. He also initiated a neighborhood-driven continuing-education model that couples online courses with in-person "learning circles" that meet at local library branches.

Dori Roberts, from Fredericksburg, VA, is the founder and CEO of Engineering for Kids, a company spearheading the spread of technology clubs for children and youth. Roberts saw the power of engaging students in STEM (science, technology, engineering, and mathematics) subjects through fun, hands-on activities. Her Engineering for Kids clubs are now in more than 140 locations in 33 states and 23 countries, and she continues to develop new lessons that allow students from ages 4 to 14 to explore everything from outer space to the depths of the sea. The newest "Junior Engineers" segment, for kids aged between four and six, is currently her fastest-growing program.

Connecting Distant and Unexpected Concepts

These creative individuals and many more like them foster new neural bonds that enable more connections between concepts. The more connections one has between ideas, the more likely one will be to deliver new and creative results. For example, the idea to blend data storage and DNA might sound a bit weird, but it's exactly the way creativity works. Connecting concepts, even if they're disparate and seemingly unrelated, is the essence of the type of creative cognitive processing called divergent thinking.[6] The ability to generate novel ideas by exploring off-the-wall connections and unexpected solutions is exactly the opposite of more common convergent thinking, which follows a particular set of logical steps to arrive at one "correct" solution.

It's not always easy to deviate from the norm or break from the pack, and it's been noted that the most creative people are also often the most confident, independent, daring, intuitive, and flexible. Super-creative types often possess the courage to take risks, make waves, challenge traditions, and "bend a few rules" – all requisite traits when one works with incomplete ideas, where relevant facts are missing, rules are cloudy, and "correct" procedures are non-existent.[7]

Creativity may also be viewed as a sort of eruption, following a sudden association of concepts. That's why some refer metaphorically to the creative act as "quantum leap thinking," analogous to an electron changing its orbit while generating or absorbing a quantum of energy.[8]

The Joy of Creativity and the Creativity of Joy

Being creative doesn't at all mean being exclusively happy. It can be difficult. Obstacles and adversities can pile up, and prevailing skepticism can weigh you down. Successful social or business innovators often report that their first years of effort were a strain on their resources and relationships. Yet they persisted, compelled by an idea, a vision, and, in many cases, a mission to support the disadvantaged and help others to thrive.

The creative process can be tough. But as the quotes at the beginning of this chapter suggest, creative people are alike in one respect: they all love what they do. This suggests that even in the face of adversity, creativity is

---

[6] Guilford (1950); Runco (2007).
[7] See Davis (1993).
[8] Mapes (2003).

a truly joyful experience. And more importantly, the reverse is true: joy stimulates creativity. That's right: joy and play create more connections between neurons, particularly in the frontal lobe, the part of the brain responsible for higher, uniquely human mental functions. What we have, in fact, is a positive feedback loop between joy and creativity. Creative acts, particularly moments of inspiration or "a-ha" moments, deliver a feeling of joy, whereas joy stimulates the brain plasticity essential for creativity.[9] And critical to both states are certain wonder chemicals called neurotransmitters.

Happy Neuro-connectors

Many neuro-hormones serve as neurotransmitters, connecting more distant neuronal synapses. But two in particular enhance our creativity by making it a joyful experience. They are dopamine and endorphins.

Dopamine influences the formation of new neurons, which, as we know, increases brain plasticity. Dopamine also influences our appetite for novelty and creative drive. It's associated with pleasure and is considered a factor contributing to a divergent mind.[10]

Endorphins serve as a brain-controlled painkillers. They also deliver the feeling of pleasure and even euphoria.[11]

While dopamine gives a long-lasting feeling of joy, endorphins' effects last only for a short time, delivering a brief but noticeable "kick" of pleasure. The happy result is that creative individuals are both rewarded short-term for their efforts (endorphins) and invited to continue the "creative drive" for more lasting pleasure (dopamine).[12]

The Whole Brain

Brain plasticity plays a cardinal role in opening the mind. It's an intrinsic property of the brain, regardless of age, enabling the nervous system to adapt to environmental pressures, physiologic changes, and experiences.[13] This property is fundamental to the adaptability of our behavior, learning and memory processes, brain development, and brain repair.[14]

[9] Pellis and Pellis (2009).
[10] Flaherty (2005); Chermahini and Hommel (2010); Kaufman (2010); Beversdorf (2013).
[11] Hawkes (1992); Scheve (2014); Stoppler (2014).
[12] Sprouse-Blum et al. (2010); Rusu (2013).
[13] Pascual-Leone et al. (2005, 2011).
[14] Sale et al. (2014).

It's important to understand that creativity doesn't happen in just one part of the brain, and that IQ is not what determines our ability to be creative. Instead, the creative process draws on the whole brain and all the neural connections continually being made there. In the 1960s, it was Frank Barron[15] who discovered that creativity is a dynamic interplay of many different brain regions, emotions, and our unconscious and conscious processing systems. It's fueled by a complex assortment of intellectual, emotional, motivational, and moral characteristics.

Creative people have a preference for complexity and ambiguity, as we will see in the next chapter. They also have an unusually high tolerance for chaos, and they know how to harness chaos into the process of generating new order.

Creativity Fosters Wonder-Making

> Creativity involves breaking out of established patterns in order to look at things in a different way. (Edward de Bono)

Given creativity's complexity, we shouldn't be too surprised to learn that the "gnarliness" of the challenge itself can spur creative drive. In other words, simply taking the step to address an insurmountable yet pressing problem may be a source of satisfaction in and of itself, as the "smart" brain derives joy and pleasure from the process of generating novel ideas. Creative people tap into a strong source of internal satisfaction when pursuing the "impossible," and have a strong motivation to perceive it as possible. This explains why a higher level of possibilitivity becomes, for creative people, an endless source of pleasure and satisfaction.

Take for example the African physics teacher who addressed seemingly unsolvable issues of education, pollution, and energy production. Not only was he able to use divergent thinking to come up with a novel solution, the process, despite innumerable obstacles, was so satisfying that he's continued to expand his project, involving other teachers and reaching other regions of Africa.

---

[15] Barron (1968).

CHAPTER 13

Complexity, Inconsistent Thinking, and Paradoxes

> What we agree with leaves us inactive, but contradiction makes us productive. (Johann Wolfgang von Goethe)
>
> One is fruitful only at the cost of being rich in contradictions. (Friedrich Nietzsche, *Twilight of the Idols*)

In Chapter 6 we mentioned the powerful need to maintain a consistent concept of oneself, other people, and the world. Some researchers say this quest for cognitive closure is often associated with the desire for predictability, a preference for order and structure, and discomfort with ambiguity or indecisiveness.

Cognitive consistency is also considered a key feature of critical thinking, along with clarity, precision, accuracy, relevance, logical correctness, completeness, and fairness. We often perceive inconsistencies as negative – a consequence of ignorance or lazy thinking or excessive emotion.[1] And our minds work overtime to smooth out any wrinkles of mismatched thought. So what did Goethe and Nietzsche mean when they gave us those words quoted above? Why did Goethe say that contradiction makes us productive and Nietzsche indicate that one is fruitful only at the cost of being rich in contradictions? If they're right then perhaps we should all make a U-turn and consider the importance of cognitive inconsistencies and contradictions as tools for achieving our dreams. Here's a good story to get us on our way.

During the second Gulf War, the American general Stanley McChrystal did the most inconsistent thing imaginable: in the midst of battle, he completely reshaped his army's structure, decentralizing authority and building self-organizing teams. With troops on the ground confronting the enemy, General McChrystal discarded centuries of conventional, top-down

---

[1] See, for example, http://changingminds.org/disciplines/argument/fallacies/logical_inconsistency.htm (retrieved March 16, 2019).

management wisdom and remade his military task force into a horizontal network of semi-autonomous groups. The soldiers were told to take matters into their own hands and figure out the best solutions. Perhaps even more astonishing is that they did so and won easily. It worked because those most directly engaged in the conflict were able to communicate directly with each other and come up with the most appropriate solution in any given circumstance. McChrystal's insights from this success were the inspiration for his book *Team of Teams*,[2] which looks at complexity management and the potentially positive effects of admitting some chaos into "logical" and "well-planned" operations, be it in battle or business.

Chaos May Help

McChrystal replaced traditional top-down structure with decentralized management believing that a more "chaotic" organization would be more nimble – that if soldiers interacting on the battlefield were free to come up with bottom-up decisions, they would be better able to handle situations as they arose.

This is a great example of complexity theory, which suggests that free interaction among individuals or groups creates feedback loops that in turn create unexpected entities on a higher order (like audience members whose applause is out of sync at first but who gradually begin to clap in rhythmic unison; or birds taking off in chaotic disarray before assembling in a V-shaped formation). The traditional A to B, B to C thinking becomes inapplicable, as A interacts freely with B, B influences C, and C cooperates with A, and out of these feedback loops comes unified function without direct leadership. Likewise, Gulf War battle logistics, instead of being orchestrated from the top down, emerged out of seemingly chaotic interactions among the soldiers.

To get to the best possible decisions, General McChrystal had to be able to see the positive side of chaos – that people "at the bottom," if freely interacting, could come up with the best solutions because they're closest to the problems. Many business and social leaders use the same tactics (remember Ricardo Semler from Chapter 1). By rejecting a traditional management culture that trains us to view chaos as a negative source of disintegration and a synonym for "mess," they empower teams and individuals to develop their own novel ideas.

---

[2] McChrystal (2015).

Of course we're not talking about a "let it go" laissez-faire attitude here. Some preconditions must be set to ensure that "chaos" leads to a desirable, rather than destructive, outcome.[3] Instead, I suggest that by introducing a paradigm of "free interaction of elements" into one's thought, one opens a gateway to "complexity as a way of thinking"[4] and the generation of creative ideas.

Another exciting aspect of "complexity thinking" is that it can foster those sudden jumps we recognize as "a-ha" moments. Freely interacting elements, through multiple feedback loops and mutual reinforcement, can suddenly generate an emergent, novel entity. Let's imagine, for example, a group of friends hanging out, having a good time and tossing out "crazy" ideas before laughing them off. Then suddenly, one idea doesn't sound so nuts. Sure it's a little weird. But it's new, it's different, and you know, it just might work. And there, unexpectedly and out of the "chaos" of social interaction, is the seed of a new business venture.

It will come as no surprise that many startups have been conceived in similar fashion. Take Uber's ride-sharing service for example. Its founders were hanging out in Paris in 2008, listening to some good music and having a few beers until it was time to head home and they couldn't find a taxi. They began talking about the taxi problem and over the course of several hours came up with the framework for an online service to solve it.[5]

Or consider Warby Parker. Four friends, while at Wharton Business School, had an idea to make quality eyewear affordable and accessible, and a company was born.[6] Similarly, the Thrillist,[7] an online media brand covering food, drink, travel, and entertainment in the United States and Great Britain, was conceived when its founders, Ben Lerer and Adam Rich, were sitting on a roof, drinking beer and chatting. A conversation about where one of them might take his girlfriend for dinner led to the idea of an online platform to help other men in similar situations. And of course there's Mark Zuckerberg, who disclosed that as a teenager, he and his Harvard roommates got the idea of FaceMash, the predecessor to Facebook, after a night of partying.[8]

---

[3] More about this in my previous book, *Empowering Leadership of Tomorrow* (Praszkier, 2018).

[4] Caption from Axelrod and Cohen's book, *Harnessing Complexity* (2000, p. 28).

[5] See https://mic.com/articles/83175/7-successful-businesses-started-over-a-couple-of-beers#.YtCLwr YGJ (retrieved March 16, 2019).

[6] From one of the co-founders speech, see www.zdnet.com/article/warby-parker-co-founder-neil-blumenthal-dishes-on-the-eyewear-companys-sudden-success (retrieved March 16, 2019).

[7] See www.thrillist.com (retrieved March 16, 2019).

[8] Launched in 2003; see www.rollingstone.com/culture/news/the-battle-for-facebook-20100915 (retrieved March 16, 2019).

The Black Swan Metaphor

> I suspect that they put Socrates to death because there is something terribly unattractive, alienating, and nonhuman in thinking with too much clarity. (Nassim Nicholas Taleb)

In 2007 Nassim Taleb published his book *The Black Swan*,[9] named for the metaphor that describes improbable events that come as a surprise, have an immense impact, and are often inappropriately rationalized after the fact with the overuse of hindsight. Since then, this metaphor has gained traction as a way to understand the contemporary world.

Black swan events are another form of chaos or inconsistency. They are by definition unpredictable. If an event can be foreseen through mathematical or logical thought, it doesn't qualify.

However, Albert Einstein, Carl Gustav Jung, and, more recently, Nobel laureate Daniel Kahneman (author of *Thinking Fast and Slow*)[10] have suggested that intuitive thinking (*fast thinking*, according to Kahneman) may help us predict events that otherwise are non-predictable. Intuition enables one to draw on thousands of hours of previous experience to arrive at one "a-ha" moment. It's a vital counterpart to slow, logical thought. And our friend imagination serves to facilitate the interplay between the two. We'll take a closer look at the role of imagination in the next section. But it's fair to say that German philosopher Immanuel Kant hit the nail on the head when he said that imagination plays the central role in harmonizing intuition and logical thinking.[11]

Examples of negative black swans include technical disasters, such as the sinking of the Titanic (1912) or the tsunami nuclear accident in Fukushima (2011). Some may relate to the consequences of economic "bubbles" like the dot-com crash (2000–2) and the fall of Lehman Brothers (2008), which triggered a worldwide recession. But black swans can also move us forward. Ground-breaking scientific advancements, such as Einstein's relativity theory (1905) or quantum theory (late nineteenth to early twentieth centuries), would certainly fall into this category, as would major social innovations. Mohammad Yunus's introduction of the microcredit banking system for the poor is a good example. Events such as these were unpredictable in a lineal, logical way. But could we possibly use intuition and imagination to foresee comparable events in the future? What about peace

---

[9] Taleb (2010).
[10] Kahneman (2011).
[11] After Fritz and Werther (2013).

in the Middle East pursued by the Israeli–Saudi-Arabian coalition? Or an emergence of an acceptable unified field theory in physics? Or discovery of life somewhere in the space? Perhaps in the future we may know more.

Creative Contradictions

Generating new ideas and being creative is not at all logical, concludes Roger von Oech, a well-known author specializing in creative thinking.[12] Why not? Because to be creative, one has to continuously contradict oneself through:

- Having knowledge but often relying on intuition instead.
- Seeing unexpected, unusual connections while remaining sane and not having a mental disorder.
- Working hard but also spending time doing nothing.
- Generating many ideas, most of which are useless.
- Looking at the same thing as everyone else yet seeing something different.
- Desiring success but learning how to fail (and learning from failures).
- Being persistent but not stubborn.
- Listening to experts but knowing how to disregard them.

In business, contradictions that foster creativity are even more extreme. According to the *Harvard Business Review*,[13] creative leaders should, for example:

- Affirm each person's need for individual recognition and identity yet also tend to the needs of the collective.
- Mix patience and a sense of urgency.
- Balance bottom-up initiatives and top-down interventions.

So, must creative people turn their backs on traditional and "predictable" A to B, B to C thinking? Does innovation pop up only in contradictory environments? This was a topic of research carried out by a respected American psychology professor, Mihály Csíkszentmihályi, who interviewed dozens of leading innovators from diverse disciplines. One of his conclusions was that creative individuals have "antithetical traits."[14] For example:

- They have a great deal of physical energy, but are often quiet and at rest.
- They enjoy and practice playfulness, but also strict discipline.

---

[12] One of his book's chapter titles (von Oech, 2008, p. 37).
[13] See Hill et al. (2014).
[14] Csíkszentmihályi (1997a, pp. 58–76).

- They alternate between imagination and fantasy at one end and a rooted sense of reality at the other.
- They merge opposite tendencies on the continuum between extroversion and introversion (which is unusual, as psychologists hold that being either an extrovert or an introvert is a stable personality trait).
- They are remarkably humble and proud at the same time.
- They have both a rebellious streak and a strong culture of basic (traditional) points of reference.
- They are passionate about their work and objective about it as well.

All these traits indicate that living in a universe of contradictions probably keeps the mind in a specific mode of readiness to jump to new concepts and to merge distant ideas (divergent thinking). Living with logical gaps, metaphorically, tackles our brain's plasticity, putting the avalanche of new neural connection on alert and ready to break free.

Insightful Role of Paradoxes

This title sounds like an oxymoron by itself. Paradoxes don't generally clarify and illuminate; we usually think of them as obscuring reality and aggravating our apprehension. But not so fast. Consider the following hypothetical scenario:

While driving to your office you see a bumper sticker on the car in front of you that reads:

My convictions are not for public display.

What the hell? This guy is publicly displaying his conviction that his convictions are not for public display, completely contradicting himself. As you continue your drive you wrestle with the inconsistency you just encountered.

Later at the office, the bumper sticker keeps popping up in your mind, inviting other odd thoughts. You recall an old Groucho Marks quote that goes something like:

Outside of a dog, a book is a man's best friend; inside of a dog, it's too dark to read.

This amuses and also bothers you. What a ridiculous thought. And why is it occurring to you now? Surrounded by office colleagues, you chuckle discretely at the absurdity of it all.

Later that morning, you're in a marketing meeting. The issue on the table is how to increase sales through your company's online apps by making them more user-friendly. You can't stop thinking about contradictions – the bumper sticker and the inside of the dog. At some point you have a weird thought: maybe we should make a promotion campaign criticizing our own products? What an oxymoron: marketing through self-criticism! You laugh, and people stare at you. It seems that after this meeting you'll be clearing out your desk. "Bring in the pall bearers," you think. And instantly you recall Yogi Berra saying:

> *Always go to other people's funerals, otherwise they won't come to yours.*

You crack up and say, "Why don't we launch a well-publicized competition with great incentives for customers who find bugs and deficiencies in our apps? We'll stand out with a provocative marketing message. We'll motivate our audience to diligently use and analyze our products. We'll turn critics into supporters by pulling them to our side, inviting them to share their opinions with us, and taking them seriously. We'll build mutual trust. We'll create a great marketing tool and attract media attention with a barnstorming finale complete with prizes, music and celebrities. And we'll get useful feedback we can use to improve our products while positioning ourselves as a customer-centered company."

It takes a minute for everyone to process such a bold concept, but they love it. You've solved a host of challenges with one creative idea by allowing your mind to play with atypical associations and contradictions. The paradoxes you puzzled over earlier in the day became wedges working their way into traditional, A-to-B thinking and creating an opening for an unconventional and creative idea.

It's for good reason that philosophers favor paradoxes. It was Eubulides of Miletus, back in the fourth century BC, who coined the famous liar paradox:

> *Consider the statement of a liar who declares "everything I say is false." If he is indeed lying, then he is telling the truth, which means he is lying. If he is lying than he is telling the truth that he is lying, so he is not lying.*

Another philosopher, Karl Popper, wrote to his friend the following letter:

> *Dear M. G.,*
>
> *Kindly return this card to me but make sure to mark "Yes," or to put some other mark of your choice, in the black rectangle to the left of my signature if, and only if, you feel justified in predicting that, upon its return, I shall find this space empty.*
>
>   *Yours sincerely*
>   *K. R. Popper*

If Popper's friend sends it blank then he should check it, as the requirement is to mark it if it will arrive blank. However, if he checks it then it means that he is sure that this spot will arrive blank, so it shouldn't be marked.

These and other paradoxes help break the brain out of its routine, disrupting cognitive patterns by establishing contradictory circumstances that set the stage for something new and encourage divergent thinking. Of course convergent cognition has its place, and sometimes logical, cohesive thought is required. It's up to us to recognize the alternatives before us, choose what is appropriate for the situation, and even have a little fun with the options. Paradoxes may not always be of direct help, but they can still offer indirect benefit by helping the mind relax between challenges.

Inconsistencies Pave the Way for Working Wonders

As our hypothetical example shows, inconsistent thinking can be a boon in business. One startup founder[15] said that the success of a new venture might be dependent on a willingness to embrace inconsistency and contradict oneself. And Jeff Bezos, the entrepreneur, investor, and computer scientist best known as the founding CEO of Amazon, has said that people who are usually right frequently change their minds, and consistency of thought is not at all a particularly positive trait. He encourages leaders to challenge themselves with ideas that contradict previous convictions.[16]

While cognitive consistency is and will remain the default and dominant trend of our minds, admitting inconsistencies and opening our thoughts to complexity, chaos, jumps of thought, and paradoxes could be, in part, what enables us to see what is perceived by others as weird, unrealizable, or impossible as utterly attainable. Inconsistencies may be one of the keys to Working Wonders.

---

[15] Joel Gascoigne, Buffer, https://buffer.com/, see http://joel.is/want-to-be-successful-be-inconsistent/ (both retrieved March 16, 2019).

[16] See https://signalvnoise.com/posts/3289-some-advice-from-jeff-bezos (retrieved March 16, 2019).

CHAPTER 14

Minority Influence

Humanistic Psychiatry: From a Minority Group to Majority Transformation

In the 1970s, I was a member of an alternative mental health group called Synapsis, which worked to humanize psychiatry in Poland. At that time the predominant model of mental health was strictly biological, grounded in the organic (genetic and anatomic) etiology of human disorders dealt with solely through medical treatment.

We were a small group of a dozen professionals and lay-therapists and a dozen or so student volunteers. Our leader united us around such values as human and patients' rights, in the firm belief that social context has a significant effect on both the etiology and treatment of mental disorders, and the conviction that personal relationships can be healing per se.[1]

We carried out several research projects applied to diverse target groups, documenting the significance of psychotherapy.[2] The results were published[3] and shared through the media and at professional and public meetings. And the response was visceral.

We were continually attacked by the psychiatric establishment, which latched onto the term "professional" and spread the word directly and indirectly that we weren't true professionals, even though our studies were well documented. Feeling under siege, we reaffirmed our shared bond and commitment and became even more determined to pursue our mission and promote a new, more humane approach to treating people with mental problems.

---

[1] Along with Humanistic Psychology and the teaching of American psychotherapist Carl Rogers, very well known in the 1970s; see Rogers (1995).
[2] Boys diagnosed with personality disorders, neurotic clients as well as with schizophrenic patients and their families.
[3] Both studies were published in English, as these were Polish-American projects partnering with NIMH USA (see Jankowski et al., 1975, 1976).

As a consolidated and mobilized minority, we spoke the same jargon, shared the same beliefs, and socialized and partied together. We argued for the same values, read the same books, and shared consistent concepts. We also had a strong feeling of identity, empowering us to stand up against the mainstream establishment. We understood that we needed the freedom and flexibility to get the message out and gain buy-in from other professionals. In this spirit we engaged mainstream organizations,[4] presenting our findings at professional conferences in the hope that our minority would influence the majority.

Early on we managed to sway some important figures, including the director of a big psychiatric hospital, who went through our training programs and agreed to endorse our method. In return, we supported his efforts to transform his struggling hospital into a more open and humane institution, significantly shortening patients' length of stay and adding psycho-social treatment methods to medical protocols. This hospital became a model for similar facilities, and within a few years, our approach was widely adopted by mental health institutions, became part of legislation related to psychiatric care, and gained acceptance in the mainstream medical community.

Those years of struggle gave me a strong feeling of identity with my team and the values we shared, which at that time did a lot for my personal development. And the success we ultimately achieved made me feel like I could fly.

Bubbles of New in the Sea of Old

Why do I share that story? Because it's a great example of another means of idea generation called the bubbles theory.[5] Using the metaphor of gas bubbles forming in water as it heats, researchers have described "bubbles of new" that appear and diffuse in the "sea of old." One first observes a nucleus of small "bubbles of new," which connect together, grow in size, and become large, full-blown bubbles that eventually break through the surface. Bubbles may be interpreted as forerunners of change in societies undergoing transition. As the change progresses, islands of "new" gradually expand at the expense of the "old."

According to the bubble theory, leaders are of central importance, especially at the beginning of a minority-driven transition. They sow the seeds

---

[4] E.g., the Polish Psychiatric Association.
[5] Introduced by professors Andrzej Nowak and Robin Vallacher who modeled on a computer the diffusion of novel ideas; see Nowak and Vallacher (2005); Vallacher and Nowak (2007).

of the "new" and help the minority withstand the pressure of the majority during early stages of change. They can also foster connections among isolated clusters of "new," which become channels for the diffusion of the idea.

This is what happened with our Synapsis group in the 1970s. We were a bubble of new, gaining allies in various places (new bubbles), and we kept all the bubbles well connected through our meetings, conferences, training programs, etc. Throughout, our leader provided strong support, especially in the face of resistance, introducing new mental health concepts, and serving as mentor, teacher, and community builder.

The bubbles of new grew, connected, and, over time, contributed to significant change that could be compared to the phenomenon of phase transition in physics, like when water heated to a temperature of 212°F transforms into gas.

Casting Doubts

Minorities influence majorities by casting doubt, and by presenting a cohesive stance, adamant commitment, and strong evidence. They induce conversions by changing personal beliefs, which leads to changes in behavior. And not surprisingly, their first converts are usually those who complied with the majority, without truly believing in its objectives. By finding smart ways to engage the attention of the majority and coherently express its alternative views, the minority can reinforce its own identity, gaining strength and unity through the process and making a strong impression.[6]

Consistency or Flexibility?

Some academicians say that consistency in a minority's message is key to influencing the majority. Consistency bolsters the impression that the minority is right and that its members are committed to their viewpoint. Advocates of this view claim that when confronted with a consistent opposition, members of the majority will ultimately be compelled to rethink their position.

However, other researchers highlight the importance of flexibility and question the value of consistency. They argue that the minority needs to adjust its messaging so it reaches diverse segments of the majority. Also, flexibility counters the majority's attempts to paint the minority as rigid,

[6] Moscovici (1976); De Drue and De Vries (2001); Nemeth and Goncalo (2005).

dogmatic, and intolerant. Moreover, flexibility welcomes potential partners, and new alliances and conversations can help erode the majority's view, as more people say "Well, they made a good point there, let's give it some more thought."

Creative Minority and Possibilitivity

The famous British historian Arnold Toynbee extolled the degree to which minorities contribute to innovation, claiming that it was the creativity of the minorities that made America great. He called those minority innovators "aristocrats," giving them parity with aristocrats by blood.[7]

In fact, research confirms that minority members are, by their mere position, often stimulated to find new solutions to problems, while members of the majority idly enjoy their mainstream arrangements. Interestingly, this very dynamic is a current topic of conversation on Facebook (2017). On a blog called Creative Minorities Initiative,[8] you can find a call for a Young Muslim Leaders Summit titled "Turning Your Passions into Possibilities." Online there are articles about Jews being a minority in Babylon and Jeremiah coming up with novel solutions that consolidated them as a Diaspora,[9] and about the Catholic minority in Protestant Holland being the vehicle for innovations and creativity.[10] In history and in the future, minorities are a creative force for change.

In my work with Synapsis, I remember how creative we were in our efforts to find atypical ways to get our message to mainstream professionals and the public at large. We considered several research methodologies to make our case evidence-based beyond any doubt. We thought about inviting mainstream doctors to our therapy sessions as observers, organizing public debates, writing articles in popular magazines, sneaking into "their" professional publications, letting our ex-patients tell their stories, and much more.

On top of that, we simply had the feeling that we could do it ourselves – our small group of a few dozen professionals and students could change the predominant system. Looking back, I can say without a doubt that our identification as the minority increased our possibilitivity.

---

[7] Toynbee (1962).

[8] See www.facebook.com/CMILosAngeles (retrieved March 16, 2019).

[9] See, for example, www.firstthings.com/article/2014/01/on-creative-minorities (retrieved March 16, 2019).

[10] See www.catholicworldreport.com/2017/10/03/dutch-cardinal-dont-underestimate-power-of-catholics-as-a-creative-minority/ (retrieved March 16, 2019).

CHAPTER 15

Networks That Boost Creativity

I was trained to be well-organized; to rely solely on diligent pre-planning and leave nothing to chance. I also frequently heard that "success is no coincidence." So the revelation that some discoveries come without fore-thought, and that casual encounters can be fortuitous, spontaneously boosting creativity and enhancing performance, came as a shock to me.

In fact, some of our most familiar and useful products came about purely by accident. Velcro, penicillin, X-rays, Teflon, dynamite, Post-it Notes, corn flakes, and the theory of gravitation, are but a few examples. Such unexpected discovery and fortunate happenstance is called *serendipity* (a name based on an old Persian fairy tale, "The Three Princes of Serendip," about three princes who were always making accidental discoveries).[1] It happens all the time, even to dedicated planners. And those interested in creativity and the generation of new ideas welcome it, even nourish and cultivate it. But how can you cultivate something that is by definition random and uncontrollable? Managing the unpredictable sounds like an oxymoron. It may well be, but some (especially in Silicon Valley) counter that while you can't influence the generation of unplanned ideas directly, you can create an environment that fosters them.[2]

Accidental Encounters

A good example of this is a story of two pharmaceutical companies.[3] One was a stable behemoth, skillfully but traditionally managed. The other was undergoing a period of upheaval, in which construction related to asbestos mitigation required that employees be dislodged from their

---

[1] Roberts (1989); Andel (1994).
[2] Lindsay (2014).
[3] Lindsay (2014).

offices and moved to interim locations. Guess which company generated more innovations, had more patents, and published more papers during that time: it was the one experiencing relative "chaos." A study revealed that communication between employees in the "stable" company was more or less structured, occurring as a top-down interaction. Whereas, at the company in turmoil, employees were shuffled to new places where they had random encounters with associates from various departments and of diverse management levels – people they wouldn't have otherwise met. It turns out that these accidental meetings generated a flurry of creative activity and serendipitous discoveries. Typically siloed employees got booster shots of inspiration, as they had new encounters and teamed up with new partners to generate ideas through peer-to-peer collaboration.

Similarly, after a decline in productivity following Yahoo's implementation of a work-from-home policy, the new CEO at the time (Marissa Mayer) called employees back to the office, convinced that working solo caused declines in creativity and random connectivity would stimulate it. To encourage that connection Mayer created a comfortable, centrally located gathering space around the coffee machine, inviting people to linger and exchange ideas. Along the same lines, Yahoo, Google, Facebook, and other companies have all worked to encourage serendipity, commissioning new campuses expressly designed to maximize casual meetings among employees and spark innovation. For example, Google's HR leader Laszlo Bock wrote a book showing the many benefits of a high freedom culture.[4]

Horizontal and Diagonal Communication and Informal Networks

Whether intentionally created or not, these fertile environments foster a specific kind of connection known as *horizontal* (among colleagues and peers at the same level) and *diagonal* (between different levels and departments). It goes without saying that both types of connection can be efficient ways to communicate across departments and management levels,[5]

---

[4] Bock (2015).
[5] See, for example, http://smallbusiness.chron.com/importance-diagonal-communication-routes-35496 .html or http://yourbusiness.azcentral.com/difference-diagonal-horizontal-flow-communication-17341.html (both retrieved March 16, 2019).

especially in modern business environments, where projects often require the cooperative efforts of more than one department and associates from various levels.[6] Diagonal or horizontal communication routes allow the nimble sharing of information directly, rather than according to a strict vertical hierarchy, which can slow down the information exchange and gum up the proverbial works. Information is shared through informal discussions, phone calls, social media, casual meetings over the lunch break, and social activity, without being hampered by chain-of-command requirements. And the result can be mutual inspiration and new opportunities for unexpected cooperation.

Generally, any kind of informal network can become a lever for generating new ideas and establishing new value-added cooperation. In companies such as Semco, as we saw in Chapter 1, employees often come up with new concepts in casual encounters. These ideas become projects, attract teams and, at the end of the day, might generate a new product. In the absence of an imposed structure, new thought, new ideas, and new collaborations take shape with serendipitous results.

Interestingly, in such situations, individual traits don't seem to matter much. At Google a project called Aristotle, spanning many years, documented that neither the IQ nor experience level of individual group members had any influence on a group's performance. The final revelation was that what really matters are features unrelated to the individuals, but rather to group norms. Especially important is the psychological safety of the team members; it's essential to create a space where they feel comfortable and safe enough to not only focus on the task at hand, but also to share personal information, such as details of health or family problems. The second crucial factor is that each group member should speak for roughly the same amount of time in total (though they may speak for varying periods of time in particular meetings).[7]

Within these basic parameters, random and informal meetings can become a hotbed of productivity and innovation. As a result, we can conclude that serendipity is totally "democratic," available to anyone, especially when it comes to working groups, and depending only on the way participants shape their norms and communication channels.

---

[6] See, for example, Darbellay et al. (2014).
[7] Duhigg (2016).

New Architecture: Tearing Down the Walls Between Disciplines

> As an architect you design for the present, with an awareness of the past, for a future which is essentially unknown. (Norman Foster)

Horizontal and diagonal connectivity across departments, disciplines, and management levels has become a hot issue among architects challenged to design office space to boost serendipity.[8]

In-depth interviews[9] and studies show that architects believe that well-designed spaces can play an essential role in innovation and the incubation of new products and ideas, and they're applying creative spatial strategies to stimulate mixing and collaboration among people and across disciplines. They're replacing standard offices with buildings and rooms that encourage face-to-face communication and collaboration, and even tearing down the walls between the offices of various tenants, such as between a university and a business, to enable connections between different "universes" for mutual inspiration and the creation of new ideas.

Architects designing with serendipitous connections in mind are also involving employees, inviting them to contribute to modeling their own spaces to support their needs. Call it the "democratization" of innovation.

An example of this is architect Frank Gehry's Stata Center at the Massachusetts Institute of Technology. The building accommodates multiple disciplines, provides spaces for working in the open, and incorporates transition zones such as hallways and staircases as places for spontaneous encounters. While space for work that requires privacy and quiet is set apart from common areas, these large, interactive spaces full of natural light encourage expansive thinking. After all, those who spend all their time in a box will find it difficult to think outside of it.

A similar approach can be found at Google in Zurich.[10] Their research revealed that the optimal working environment for Zooglers (as Google employees in Zurich are fondly referred to) should be diverse and, at the same time, harmonious. It should be fun and enjoyable, and also create opportunities for relaxation, which is crucial for stimulating creative thinking.

---

[8] Lange (2016).
[9] Wagner and Watch (2017).
[10] See Google EMEA Engineering Hub (2009).

In that vein, communal areas are intentionally dispersed throughout the building, to encourage Zooglers to circulate throughout the floors and enhance communication between the different working groups and teams.[11]

The Power of Weak Connections

Once we understand how fostering communication networks can enhance their effectiveness, it's reasonable to assume that the most powerful and supportive connections would be strong, durable bonds we've formed over time, especially with family or close friends. In fact, research shows the opposite is true. Strongly bonded individuals do form close-knit circles. And while the members of those cliques are indeed sharing resources and supporting each other, these resources tend to saturate at some point, as the closed circles are cut off from myriad other resources and relationships.

Connections that proved more helpful were weaker associations made outside of close-knit clusters. Mark Granovetter's famous research in the 1960s[12] (since repeated in various settings) documented how the connections that proved most effective in conducting a job search were not close friends but distant acquaintances. Moreover, weak ties not only gave individuals greater job opportunities, but also helped them retain those jobs in the long term (compared to those who found work through connections to strong bonds).

This discovery led to the concept of *the strength of weak ties*. These weak bonds become crucial bridges between members of closely knit circles and the resources available outside the cluster. Even if only one group member has a weak relationship with someone from a distant group, he or she automatically provides a connection for all members of both groups. In Granovetter's concept, weak ties are far more likely than strong ones to bridge gaps between groups.[13]

Conversely, a lack of weak ties deprives the group of information from distant parts of the social system and limits the flow of information to provincial news and the views of friends. The group becomes isolated from new ideas, trends, and options, including those of a diverse labor market.

---

[11] See Google Center in Zurich: large free spaces and areas for concentration, relax and withdrawal at www.archdaily.com/41400/google-emea-engineering-hub-camezind-evolution (retrieved March 16, 2019).

[12] See Granovetter (1973, 1983, 1995).

[13] Darling (2010); Sandstrom and Dunn (2014); also interesting to see Uhlig (n.d.).

Especially interesting for our topic of possibilitivity is Granovetter's assertion that establishing weak links requires cognitive flexibility and empathy. He also notes that weak ties have a special role in a person's propensity for social mobility. Others who've studied the subject[14] say that individuals who are prone to establishing weak connections not only have friends from wide and diverse circles, but also have a higher tolerance for varied ideas, emotions, and attitudes; they're flexible and highly adaptive to new information and unfamiliar environments.

In an earlier chapter I suggested that it's optimal to maintain a balance between strong and weak ties. Sometimes the situation requires opening to the outside world, so that previously isolated individuals, groups, or societies become connected with others through weak ties. In other cases the need is rather to come back to one's strong ties, so as to restore social identity and strength emanating from deep social and cultural roots.[15]

This means that increasing one's openness to new challenges requires, on the one hand, the propensity for initiating weak connections with diverse "universes," and on the other, striking life balance by nurturing one's roots, and thus strong bonds.

Ambience: Opening the Mind for the Impossible

It seems that we're witnessing the rise of a new kind of group. Financial technology firm Swift coined the term *innotribe* to describe these clans of creative thinkers who unite to accelerate innovation.[16]

Let's take the example of Venture Café, a nonprofit out of the Cambridge Innovation Center designed to boost innovation in the greater Boston area. Leaders of the organization believe that innovation is a social process, and see as part of their mission the need to "provide a supportive and constructive environment for conversations."[17] A visitor reported: "I've been based at the Cambridge Innovation Centre (CIC) while in Boston, and I can say with certainty that they're keen on serendipity here. Communal kitchens with shared tables and free fruit, snacks and drinks create a social environment where meeting people is easy and leads to lots of spontaneous meetings 'around the coffee machine'."[18]

---

[14] Csermely (2009).
[15] Praszkier (2012).
[16] See www.managementexchange.com/story/innotribe (retrieved March 16, 2019).
[17] See http://vencaf.org/ (retrieved March 16, 2019).
[18] See http://blog.setsquared.co.uk/2016/05/20/day-9-networking-and-serendipity (retrieved March 16, 2019).

Feeling the "tribe's" support, people are more willing to open their minds to new ideas and address unthinkable challenges. Horizontal, diagonal, and cross-disciplinary connections prep the mind for innovation; random encounters in communal spaces, and through weak connections, can bring people together to form new associations and create new thought and inspiration.

CHAPTER 16

Sync Your Mind with Others

The Mystery of Sync

My fascination with synchrony started with Steven Strogatz's book, *SYNC: How Order Emerges from Chaos in the Universe, Nature, and Daily Life*.[1] I was especially fascinated to learn of the "firefly phenomenon." Back in 1992, it was reported that fireflies in the Great Smokey Mountains blink in unison. The lightning bugs work in perfect synchrony, refraining from flashing for six seconds, then flashing exactly six times within a three-second period, then going dark for another six seconds – countless numbers of insects working together.

In Thailand, a biologist made a small experiment by capturing a bunch of fireflies and releasing them in a darkened room. After a while the insects settled down all over the walls and ceiling. At first they twinkled incoherently. Then pairs and trios began to pulse in unison. The synchronized groups grew until, finally, all of the fireflies were blinking on and off as one.

Strogatz compares fireflies to so-called "oscillators." Other examples include pacemaker cells in the human heart. About 10,000 cells generate the electrical rhythm that commands the rest of the heart cells to beat. They oscillate automatically, their voltage rising and falling in a regular rhythm, coordinating to avoid any distraction that could influence the heartbeat and cause cardiac problems. The question for scientists is: how do these 10,000 cells, with no designated leader, manage to get in sync? Especially given that no two cells are identical.[2] Strogatz claims that such synchrony is democratic, emerging out of bottom-up interaction between elements.

---

[1] Strogatz (2003).
[2] The question "how do they do it" attracted the best possible mathematicians: Albert Einstein, Henri Poincaré, Niels Bohr, and many others.

Figure 10 A v-shaped flock of birds.
Photo: Ryszard Praszkier.

After reading Strogatz and watching a YouTube video on firefly synchrony,[3] I had the sync phenomenon under my skin. I moved to observing the way birds form v-shaped flocks in flight, at one point nearly ruining a weekend getaway by continually interrupting my wife and pointing to the sky and exclaiming over another avian "v" formation.

Indeed, birds can demonstrate a remarkable ability to self-organize, taking to the sky in random chaos out of which an elegant order appears. Birds are not hierarchical, but rather take turns in the positions in the flock. They synchronize individual movements and form a pattern they can sustain for thousands of miles (see Figure 10).

To my wonderment, I found that the mystery of sync occurs everywhere, even in inanimate matter. Take for example a couple of metronomes. Put them on a wave-propagating base like a rickety desk and soon they will synchronize their rhythms. Watching a YouTube video documenting this phenomenon,[4] I came to the conclusion that there must be something in nature that makes things, animals, and humans strive for synchrony. It seemed that sync is a "preferred" state of matter. In the purview of physics, it's clear that systems in sync are at a stable energy level, and

[3] See www.youtube.com/watch?v=IBgq-_NJClo or www.youtube.com/watch?v=sROKYelaWbo (both retrieved March 16, 2019).
[4] See www.youtube.com/watch?v=W1TMZASCR-I (retrieved March 16, 2019).

self-reinforcing in their behavior. Metaphorically speaking, could this also apply to humans?

What about an audience's cacophonous applause, which suddenly synchronizes and becomes rhythmic clapping? This example gets to the heart of Strogatz's assertion that sync is democratic. Let's imagine that someone wanted to direct a group to clap in unison. This director would have to follow a predetermined script imposing a complicated process through top-down control. He or she might divide the audience into sections managed by section-officers, who would organize and control each section's clapping rhythm, which would then need to be synced with the other sections. That would take time and practice and may not work at all. Whereas a self-directed audience, using a bottom-up process, can sync within moments.

To fully appreciate the phenomenon of an audience clapping in rhythm, one must also consider the extent to which individuals differ. An extrovert, who claps fast and loud, sits close to an introvert, who, distracted by inner thoughts, claps slowly. Someone who's just been left by a girlfriend sits beside someone who's been recently married. Older audience members are next to those who are young and energized. For individuals to maintain a shared rhythm, they must connect with one another through an empathetic feedback mechanism that slows down or speeds up their own rhythm in accordance with their neighbors'. This feedback mechanism may also be crucial for the synchronization of fireflies, metronomes, and anything else that adjusts its individual movement to match that of another.

Human Sync

Have you ever sensed that your mind is synchronized with someone else's? You might describe it as having a similar vibe, or being on the same page, or feeling a sense of community. For certain joint behaviors, this coordination of minds is essential. Mating, group cohesion, or predator avoidance, for example, all depend on the brisk and correct transmission of social signals.

In such cases the neural processes in one brain are coupled with the neural processes in another brain. This process of brain-to-brain coupling looks like a wireless communication system in which two brains connect via the transmission of a signal. This is similar to the transmission of sound, during which the neural firing in the speaker's and the listener's brains exhibit joint, temporally coupled response patterns synchronizing over time.[5]

---

[5] See studies with the use of MRI (Hasson et al., 2012) and EEG (Pérez et al., 2017).

But we don't need to talk to each other to sync. Studies have shown that just staring at each other for 15 minutes is enough for two people's brains to start to synchronize. Even quietly sitting next to a partner is sufficient to generate synchrony. Often subconsciously, we synchronize ourselves to those around us, picking up subtle signals and modulating our behavior in response.[6] Sync is pervasive and even unavoidable, as individuals, small groups, or even organizations will automatically start to sync, as long as they have the freedom to create horizontal or diagonal interactions. Top-down control, if overdone, may kill this natural tendency to connect.

When we understand sync, it becomes obvious why people tend to enjoy activities such as group singing, walking in step (perhaps you've noticed your footsteps syncing with a friend's as you walk together), clapping in unison, or doing "the wave." It also becomes clear why many group activities draw on rituals with recurring elements to boost engagement and positive emotions. We're drawn to these activities because such "neural coupling" is essential to understanding others, and because they're pleasurable to us.

Being in sync means having rapport, and reducing the distance and (automatically) downplaying the differences between us. We seem to prefer the company of those whom we perceive as synchronized, because they "get us," while we're inclined to dislike those unsynchronized with us and feel misunderstood by them.[7] Metaphorically speaking, when we're in sync, a kind of "invisible energy" forms a connecting current between us and others. We can then more easily understand and relate to the other's needs or ideas, and we feel that they know what it's like to be in our shoes.

Sync Coordinates

A by-product of this union is better cooperation. It's been documented that synchrony of body movements, such as leg movements or fingertip tapping, increases cooperative reactions and interactions.[8]

This coordination is fostered by a higher level of perceived mutual understanding and, as a consequence, a strengthening social attachment among group members (which, we know, sync creates).[9] Moreover, when those who are in synchrony with us experience difficult conditions or

---

[6] Hasson et al. (2012).
[7] Sanow (2015).
[8] Wiltermuth and Heath (2009); Valdesolo and DeSteno (2011); Yun et al. (2012).
[9] Baer (2017).

challenges, they evoke more of our compassion and altruistic behavior than in asynchronous individuals. Overall, positively tuned-in group members experience improved cooperation, decreased conflict, and better performance as individuals and as a group.[10]

Sync Makes It Possible

Given all the benefits of synchronization, we can surmise that the feeling of being attuned with others sets a specific disposition to press on, explore, brainstorm, and generate new ideas. If we're out of sync, we can feel impotent and isolated, even in a group.

However, not all groups synchronize. While some operate like well-oiled machines, it's a common experience to sit in a group meeting and feel totally stuck or bored. So, what makes the difference?

Some light was shed by the Google Aristotle project (mentioned in the previous chapter), which found that groups perform well and stimulate innovation when people feel comfortable and safe enough to not only focus on the task at hand, but to also share personal information and problems, and when they feel they're able to speak for the same amount of time as the others. I would argue that these conditions serve as prerequisites for a better sync, and sync sets the group on a much more productive path.

As the "invisible energy" that provides a higher state of mutual understanding, sync serves as a supportive milieu for addressing challenges, which, in isolation, may have been perceived as unsolvable. The ability to synchronize gives us more power and makes it easier for us to see seemingly impossible things as possible.

---

[10] Barsade (2002); Reddish et al. (2013).

CHAPTER 17

Opening the Mind
Possibilitivity

So, at this point we've explored several tools we can use to dismantle the fortress of the mind and open ourselves to possibilitivity. We've looked at brain plasticity and creativity, the potential embedded in complexity and non-linear thinking, the way the minority can influence the majority and how participating in this process keeps you flexible, the power of horizontal and weak connections, and how sync and the propensity to synchronize help us see things as doable.

These preconditions are likely to create an enabling and supportive environment that primes us for success, but we can't move too far in any one direction if we want to be effective; the real magic comes in finding balance. For example, a knack for divergent (creative) thinking shouldn't oust convergent (linear) thinking, which is indispensable when it comes to solving problems of logic; and the aptitude for weaving "weak" connections shouldn't eradicate strong bonds that provide a feeling of identity and a point of reference. The real wizardry happens when we understand and can draw on the full spectrum of options and use them appropriately.

By way of example, I thought I'd wrap up Part III with a few brief stories of people who found that balance and, often against all odds, perceived their dreams and ideas as indisputably doable and achieved them.

Striking the Balance

Traveling for Ashoka, Innovators for the Public,[1] and interviewing business and social innovators, I encountered a common challenge: how to bring beneficial economic development without shattering indigenous traditional culture. For example, in June 2012, I met Karim Sy,[2] a young business and social leader from Senegal, who created Jokkolabs, a network

---

[1] As a second opinion reviewer for the Ashoka Fellowship; www.ashoka.org (retrieved March 16, 2019).
[2] See www.ashoka.org/en/fellow/karim-sy#intro (retrieved March 16, 2019).

of co-working centers,[3] designated to boost economic development in Dakar. These centers spur cooperation and mutual inspiration in communities of enterprising people who share similar values of openness and collaboration. Karim Sy sees Jokkolabs as more than working spaces. They are, in his view, a human adventure. An old African proverb goes, "If you want to walk fast, walk alone. If you want to walk far, walk with others!" Co-working space capitalized on a penchant for cooperation already embedded in the African culture and became a lever for instigating serendipity and accelerating progress, similar to the modern open-space architecture projects we've discussed. The magic of balancing old and new became the real driver of the program's success.

The balance between old and new was also a catalyst for development in some Maasai tribes. In May 2005, I went to East Africa and met with Denis Ole Sonkoi, a young Maasai activist from the Loita community located on the border of Kenya and Tanzania. He was devoted to preserving the Maasai culture and way of life but was also concerned about threats to the tribe's economic stability and subsistence. Sonkoi had a keen interest in nature and a deep pride in his Maasai heritage. He told me fascinating stories about the Maasai people, who are historically pastoral and subsist mostly on cattle husbandry. The Maasai rely on cows for food, and consider them as security in case of some disasters. But a growing variety of diseases was destroying the cows' natural healing capacities. Moreover, trading cows requires traveling to distant marketplaces, which takes many days. Fearful for his people, Sonkoi found innovative solutions to these problems.

By linking with the international organization Veterinaires Sans Frontières (Vets Without Borders), he trained paravets on the use of natural healing resources. He then organized a chain of veterinary pharmacy centers, called dawa shops, ready to intervene when needed, especially when a threat of disease was detected.

As for the livestock trading business, Sonkoi launched a buyers' association with operations closer to home. He also improved animal transportation by installing a chain of feedlots along the route to market.

All these activities were met with resistance from the elders. Sonkoi went to work convincing them that this was the right thing to do, in particular by demonstrating that all of his innovations were embedded in Maasai traditions. The elders were convinced and even accepted his village banking idea, which made it possible for the Maasai to travel without cases

---

[3] See http://jokkolabs.net/en/ (retrieved March 16, 2019).

of money. At the same time, Sonkoi also engaged the youth, training and empowering them to get involved in the new enterprises.

The best example of his efforts to balance the old and new is the burgeoning tourism industry he introduced in the region. Sonkoi launched a walking safari company that conducts tours of the Loita forest, led by the Maasai. The tours are all made on foot in order to limit tourist traffic to a sustainable level and minimize the environmental impact. The profit generated from the safari company is reinvested in the tribe's livestock trade and animal health programs. Sonkoi says that he is obsessed with achieving a healthy coexistence between the Maasai and their environment while furthering the economic sustainability of his people's traditional way of life.

In March 2005, in Kampala, I met Father Paul Okoth, who turned his own harmful childhood experience into a program to prevent domestic violence in rural areas. Okoth determined that the best option was to invest in those men who were already known perpetrators of violence. He organized a comprehensive system with men's clubs at its core. These clubs provide violence avoidance and chemical dependency counseling, as well as some economic support through small-business development training. The organization also operates an early prevention system. At the household level there are several volunteer counselors who monitor at-risk families, handle cases and, eventually, refer those in need to village counselors who are of a higher skill level. The entire system is embedded in the communities' rural social framework, balancing tradition with the most contemporary approach for prevention and counseling.

Launching a Business out of the Hospital

In March 2014, in Bangkok, I spent a few hours with Preeda Limmontakul, a candidate for the Ashoka Fellowship.[4] Although disabled and confined to a wheelchair, he radiated positive energy, telling me a story of his life that had me on the edge of my seat. Not only is he creating opportunities for people with disabilities to perform mainstream jobs as competitive equals, he is also changing public perception, showing the able-bodied that the disabled are not unfortunate souls to be pitied but competent professionals capable of significant contribution to society. He, himself, is the best example of this, and it's his life story which was for me so poignant.

---

[4] See www.ashoka.org/en/fellow/preeda-limmontakul#intro (retrieved March 16, 2019).

It starts when he was a kid and, wanting to help his parents, learned to make toys himself instead of asking his parents to buy them as other children did. After earning his undergraduate degree, he worked in and visited several factories, learning and developing his own innovative ideas. Some, like a design for a home for the aging, were in the social realm. But his most significant innovation was a redesign of the calibration system for weighing equipment. His method was well-received by many companies and saved millions of dollars in maintenance and repair costs. He also designed a training course for his system and started to write a comprehensive report on his innovation. He had completed 3 of 12 chapters when he was in a terrible car accident. He awoke in the hospital to discover that he had suffered a traumatic spinal cord injury and would never walk again. He was 29.

Limmontakul turned from despair over his condition to making plans for the future. He used his time in the hospital to develop a new business, which he launched, still from the hospital, with great success. Like many others, the business floundered during the 2008 economic crisis, but it showed that a disabled person could operate in the real world, face real competition in the market, and succeed. Limmontakul's experience ran counter to the mainstream trend of keeping disabled people in special housing and limiting their activity to simple tasks in sheltered workshops.

Inspired to shift the status quo, he formed a social enterprise, called PWD Outsource Management,[5] and launched several pilot projects. Limmontakul himself developed telemarketing software customized for callers with various physical disabilities. Within two weeks of launch, a few dozen trainees were achieving a success rate much higher than the average for telemarketing companies and generating significant profit.

Another of Limmontakul's early ideas was to train people with disabilities to monitor TV shows and report programming gaps and flaws using specially tailored software. He soon realized that information technology was the key to engaging disabled people in business. His ideas and pilot demonstrations brought public recognition for the products as well as for his objectives and served as the basis for legislation supporting mainstream employment for people with disabilities. As a result, PWD has been recognized as Thailand's first job-placement firm of its kind.

In order to shift the mindset of employers, the disabled, and the public, Limmontakul established the Will Share Association and organized training courses to teach employers how to generate profit by hiring disabled

---

[5] See http://pwdoutsourcemanagement.blogspot.com/ (retrieved March 16, 2019), only in Thai.

Figure 11 Preeda Limmontakul's coffee paintings.
Received from Preeda Limnontakul.

workers. He also developed programs for the disabled, to empower them with IT skills and self-confidence. Over time, Limmontakul's approach gained recognition, but a real breakthrough came during the major flood in Bangkok in 2011. Limmontakul led a group of disabled citizens highly skilled in IT, who played a significant role in monitoring the online platform that matched volunteers with those in need of services in the flood-affected areas. During this trying time Limmontakul also donated "coffee paintings" he made himself, to flood victims (see examples in Figure 11).[6]

Limmontakul's dream to end the public perception that people with disabilities are unfortunate victims to be pitied and see them viewed as competent, skilled professionals led him to take his ideas to the universities, tailoring their programs to suit disabled students and teachers and adding new subjects related to the empowerment of the disabled. His vision remains boundless, as he takes his training programs beyond Thailand, to other Asian-Pacific countries.

Coming back to the hospital room in that moment when Preeda Limmontakul awoke from a coma and learned about his irreparable spinal cord damage and its lifelong consequences, what was his reaction? After the initial shock, instead of despair or surrender, he chose to focus on a new business venture. Despite physical challenges and skeptical responses from those who couldn't imagine how he could run a company from a wheelchair, he was convinced that his big dream was doable. And his remarkable achievements serve as an ideal case study of possibilitivity in action.

Summary

So, with an understanding of the concept of possibilitivity and the various mechanisms that inhibit and support it, and inspiration from some amazing individuals who've accomplished what many thought impossible, we're left with the burning question of how to get more of it ourselves. How can we, in practical, everyday life build our capacity for this powerful way of being and thinking? Are there exercises – a workout of sorts – that can enhance our ability to push past skepticism and self-doubt and do the "undoable"? Can we train our brains to give us more of this "magical thinking"? Absolutely, and that's what we'll explore next.

---

[6] Photos from Preeda Limmontakul.

PART IV

Do-It-Yourself Tips

In this part we'll present several do-it-yourself (DIY) methods to help you turn theory into reality and nurture and grow your own possibilitivity. Figure 12 illustrates the elements of this part.

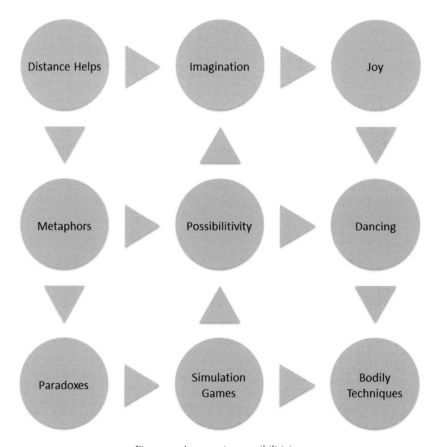

Figure 12 Augmenting possibilitivity.

CHAPTER 18

Precondition One
Building a Supportive Ambience

Social Capital

Throughout this book we've shared stories of remarkable people achieving extraordinary things. But none of them accomplished these feats alone. Each had the support of employees and colleagues providing feedback, creating new ideas, weaving supportive networks, recharging the mind's batteries, and creating a helpful environment.

The Lone Ranger syndrome is based on the false belief that if we do everything ourselves, we will get it done better, quicker, and faster. The truth is that lasting achievement in today's world requires collaboration. As leadership expert Laura Davis says, "Whether you run a company, are an educator in a school, a politician in state government, or a parent managing a family, the principle is still the same: *you must have collaboration to be successful*. And collaboration results only from quality, trusting relationships characterized by real, authentic communication."[1]

As I explored in my previous book, *Empowering Leadership of Tomorrow*, the way to harness collaborative energy is to build social capital around your idea. Basically, social capital is a blend of trust and propensity for cooperation.[2] It generates long-term endogenous (or internal) support, making the development of an idea autocatalytic, or self-sustaining – in its way, making the impossible possible.[3] Let's look at an example.

Rocky Flats Challenge

Much like this book, the title of Kim Cameron and Marc Lavine's *Making the Impossible Possible: Leading Extraordinary Performance – The*

---

[1] From www.linkedin.com/pulse/20140830152310-569986-stop-being-a-lone-ranger-and-learn-the-5-behaviors-of-a-cohesive-team/ (retrieved March 16, 2019).
[2] Coleman (1990); Putnam (1993); Adler and Kwon (2002).
[3] Burt (1997); Woolcock and Narayan (2000).

Rocky Flats Story[4] leaves no mystery as to its contents. Indeed, one of the most amazing stories of turning something "undoable" into something done is that of Rocky Flats, a nuclear plant in Colorado, which between 1952 and 1989 used plutonium to manufacture nuclear bombs. During that time, imprudence and accidents resulted in extensive radio-active contamination of the air, water, and soil in residential areas near the site. Frequent fires spread this radioactive contamination across the Denver area, making Rocky Flats arguably the greatest American nuclear pollution disaster ever.

Closed in 1992, the site created an unprecedented challenge for cleanup. The situation seemed dispiriting for the experts and deplorable for the residents. The Department of Energy calculated that the cleanup and closure of the facility would require more than 70 years (nearly three generations) and would cost at least $36 billion (more than the entire 2017 annual budget for the state of Colorado).

But to everyone's surprise and relief, Kaiser-Hill, the company that won the cleanup agreement, actually completed the entire project 60 years earlier than anticipated, and at a saving of approximately $30 billion of taxpayer money. The telling landmarks of this success were that, in 2001, Congress passed the Rocky Flats National Wildlife Refuge Act, and in 2007, the US Department of Energy transferred nearly 4,000 acres of land on the Rocky Flats site to the US Fish and Wildlife Service to establish the Rocky Flats National Wildlife Refuge,[5] where many prairie dog colonies and other wildlife thrive today.

So how did they do it? Cameron and Levine describe the heroes of their story as "positive deviants."[6] Indeed, Kaiser-Hill used what could be described as non-traditional management methods. They drew on bottom-up initiatives from empowered employees, focused on innovation, took risks and practiced visionary thinking to develop novel solutions where others failed. The authors call this practice of pursuing the best of the human condition and working to fulfill the highest potential of organizations and individuals an "abundance approach." In contrast to a "deficit approach," the abundance approach focuses on resilience, flourishing, and vitality, rather than mere goal achievement; also it is addressing abundance gaps instead of problem-solving gaps. For example,

---

[4] Cameron and Lavine (2006); Iversen (2013).
[5] See www.fws.gov/refuge/rocky_flats (retrieved March 16, 2019).
[6] For positive deviants see Dorsey (2000); Sternin (2002); Marsh et al. (2004).

instead of focusing on the path from illness to health, the abundance approach focuses on the gap between satisfactory health and vitality and flow;[7] instead of moving from being ineffective to effective, one should aim to shift from effectiveness to excellence; instead of focusing on changing relationships from harmful to helpful, one should make the leap from helpful to honoring relationships.

In general, the company achieved the impossible by engaging the entire team in positive, compelling, and charismatic visions and giving them the permission to explore, take risks, fail, and learn by failure.

Empowering Leadership

This is the kind of management it takes to make the impossible happen. In *Empowering Leadership of Tomorrow*,[8] I present the stories of leaders who have enabled bottom-up dynamics and empower individuals and groups. This sort of leadership makes a big impact through small investments, essentially creating something out of nothing. Empowering leaders enable and empower others to co-participate, co-create, and experience the joy of creativity. Staff become more committed, loyal, and innovative, believing that "I've been trusted, and things are in my hands." The collaborative search for new solutions becomes so compelling, in some cases employees don't even perceive their jobs as "work," but rather as a "game." For example, at Morning Star, one of the biggest global tomato processing companies, employees can't wait until the weekend is over and Monday comes, so they can resume their "work" playing what they call the "Tomato Game."

Like other corporations that use the Empowering Leadership approach and provide institutes that train and coach other leaders to pursue this style of management, Morning Star launched a Self-Management Institute,[9] just as Semco (as described in Chapter 1) founded Semco Style Institute[10] and LeadWise.[11]

---

[7] Flow – the mental state of with an energized focus, full involvement, and enjoyment in the process of the activity; see Csíkszentmihályi (1991).
[8] Praszkier (2018).
[9] Kirkpatrick (2011); see also http://morningstarco.com/index.cgi?Page=Self-Management (retrieved March 16, 2019).
[10] See http://semcostyle.org (retrieved March 16, 2019).
[11] See www.leadwise.co (retrieved March 16, 2019).

Unbiased Choice: Doable or Undoable

In the introduction we mentioned the Serenity Prayer:

> God, grant me the serenity
> to accept the things I cannot change,
> courage to change the things I can,
> and wisdom to know the difference.

The last plea seems crucial for this book: there are things which are obviously impossible to achieve. Since childhood I dreamed of being able to sing, tried hard, and ultimately had to give up due to complete lack of musical hearing. There are also things obviously doable; at 72, I recently learned a new style of swimming.

The essential question is how to distinguish between the two, staying open to change without "tilting at windmills." Our aim in these pages is to show you how to free the perception of doability from our biases and make decisions with a clear and objective mind.

Summary and Tips

Tip 1: Build collaborative relationships (social capital) around yourself. By growing your support networks you'll feel safer taking some risks and exploring new opportunities. It's also valuable for your groups. For example, social capital is a catalyst for economic growth. Why? Because mutual trust, the pivotal component of social capital, reinforces societal development. Higher trust yields better societal outcomes, and these, in turn, raise the level of mutual trust, which, in a feedback loop, positively influences further results.

Tip 2: As a leader, nurture and foster people's initiatives and empower your colleagues at work to take co-responsibility. This will bring jaw-dropping results; people, when granted liberty to generate and explore their ideas, are more loyal, committed, and creative. They're also more willing to take on challenges that, in a traditional top-down management structure, might be perceived as impossible.

CHAPTER 19

Forest for the Trees

Mary's Family

In my previous work as a psychotherapist, I frequently was faced with the dilemma of whether to help a client address specific symptoms or to consider these symptoms within the broader context of the client's family dynamics.[1] Some might find that distinction surprising, given that a psychotherapist's primal call is to alleviate suffering, especially when methods for doing so are readily available. So why the quandary? By way of explanation, let's look at a brief case from my practice.

Mary was a 40-year-old woman who came to me for help with symptoms of anxiety, which were particularly intense when she left home. Her husband had taken leave from his job to try to help her, and their children (10 and 12) were having problems at school. Talking with Mary I learned that that the family moved a year before, leaving behind a vicinity where they had friends and strong neighborhood connections and the children's grandparents were nearby, for a new location where they felt anonymous and isolated.

Mary's husband had been working long hours, which meant that Mary had more responsibility on the home front, but at the same time, she felt more isolated and rootless. They'd lost the bonds formed in their old neighborhood and hadn't replaced them with new ones. And as a result, Mary was struggling, the children were having problems and the family was disintegrating.

Mary's symptoms were acute, so the family's attention turned to her. Her husband worked less, helped with the household, and spent more time with the children. The kids were worried about their mother and so were better behaved. And the grandparents visited them more frequently. In a nutshell, the family reintegrated around Mary's problems. Had I focused

---

[1] Bowen (1978).

solely on alleviating Mary's anxiety, I would have contributed to a relapse, returning the family to its previous state of fragmentation. Paradoxically, it was her anxiety that glued the family back together.

So in this situation I used the Family Systems Therapy (FST) approach, which highlights an understanding of family dynamics and perception of the family as a whole system, a sort of autonomous organism.[2] In this approach, all family members, rather than just one, are invited to the session, where they are treated as a unit, just as one considers a forest rather than individual trees.

One FST technique I used was creating family genograms.[3] A genogram is a kind of family tree, serving a therapeutic purpose and including information about relationships and interactions between family members. It goes beyond a traditional genealogical map, by allowing the user to visualize hereditary patterns. A genogram captures at minimum three generations and visualizes the communication between family members, recurrent patterns, and, eventually, dysfunctions.

A genogram serves both as a diagnostic tool, enabling the outlook on the whole family context, as well as a therapeutic technique, in which drawing the family tree becomes a significant and emotional experience. Especially important for people feeling lonely and isolated, the genogram becomes a discovery experience, enabling them to regain the feeling of belonging, and identifying overlooked family members, such as a distantly located aunt, who could be a source of emotional support.

In the case of Mary's family, drawing up the genogram was an exciting experience, especially as they tracked their interactions and saw that before moving to the new location, their communication with each other had been much more lively. This led to the discussion of relationships among the family members. During subsequent family sessions Mary's symptoms, seen as a result of her isolation, became secondary and soon diminished. Mary received support through strengthened family bonds, and the family, initially weighed down with feelings of hopelessness, felt energized and empowered as they rediscovered their potential as a unit. Follow-up meetings revealed a changed family: Mary was taking computer-technology classes and working a home-based job, the kids were thriving at school, and Mary's husband had found more work–life balance – all things that had previously seemed undoable.

---

[2] Nichols (1984).
[3] McGoldrick and Gerson (1985).

Let this story serve as an example of how seeing the forest for the trees can be helpful in building up possibilitivity. Taking a step back and looking at the family system as a whole enabled seeing the significance of complex inter-relations. That perspective helped harmonize family relationships, which in turn, had a positive effect on Mary.

The More Distant the More Abstract

So does this mean distance helps in all situations? A good source for an answer is the Construal Level Theory, which says that the more distant an object is from us (spatially, temporally or socially), the more abstract our thoughts about it will be. Conversely, the closer the object is, the more concretely we will think about it. Many experiments have found that the closer we are to something, the more we focus on details and see the trees. When we step back we're better able to see the wholeness of the related issues or the forest. Let's look at a few more examples of the power of distance.

Planning an anniversary party is a fun prospect six months out. You think about the bringing family together, seeing old friends, getting a chuckle out of seeing your uncle run into his former fiancée, etc. But as the day gets closer, the more you become preoccupied with the details: how to decorate the space, what food to serve and where to buy it, where people should sit, what music to play. As the specifics of the evening come to the fore, thoughts of the overall experience of the evening fade to the background.

Or say you're meeting with co-workers to solve a pressing problem. The atmosphere is tense and the high-stakes situation takes all your attention, possibly leading to a less than desirable resolution. If, however, you go for lunch, spend a little time in nature, have some conversation with your colleagues, and, in doing so, step back from the problem, then you might see it from a more general and distant perspective and discover unexpected solutions embedded somewhere at the fringes of the issue.

Business consultants work with teams during periods of high stress, using a variety of techniques that help their clients step back and observe the problem from a distance. One of these methods is writing haiku mini-poems.

Haiku for Business

In this novel approach, the facilitator will ask the team to take a break and have everyone write a haiku mini-poem. Haiku, which comes from

Japanese tradition, juxtaposes two images or ideas, and usually has three lines and a 5-7-5-syllable rhythm.

The team members are asked to detach themselves from currently pressing issues, shift their minds to a more relaxed state, and pen a haiku. Next, each team member reads his or her poem aloud. Some of the haiku might be quite business-related:

> The corner office
> Is so much more rewarding
> With the door open.

> Simple equation
> Seeing the world through new eyes
> Equals higher pay.[4]

Others might reflect thoughts of nature:

> The sweet red roses
> Showing off their thorns proudly
> Opening their buds.[5]

> Water runs down stream.
> Fish swimming with the current.
> Life moving along.[6]

After sharing their personal haiku, the team returns to the deliberation and usually finds it much easier to find a previously latent solution that simply required stepping outside the box.

Below are a few of my haiku poems, which I wrote during times of high stress. I wrote the first one when I was offered the opportunity to take a leave from my successful career in psychotherapy and move to Ashoka, Innovators for the Public, which at that time was a frightening prospect full of unknowns:

> Around the corner
> May be roses or garbage
> Why not check it out?

The second one I wrote after I'd been with Ashoka for more than two decades and feared I wasn't making significant progress in my life:

> The tree swings and bends
> For flowing years and decades
> Imagine you there.

[4] All three from *The Business Journals* at www.bizjournals.com/bizjournals/how-to/growth-strategies/2015/09/finding-the-zen-of-business-through-haiku.html (retrieved March 16, 2019).
[5] From www.fictionpress.com/s/3125026/1/Simple-Nature-Haikus (retrieved March 16, 2019).
[6] From www.familyfriendpoems.com/poem/nature-haiku-spring (retrieved March 16, 2019).

Being at the university and under a lot of pressure to publish articles, I was questioning how much of my working life was driven by choice and how much by scholarly routine when I wrote this haiku, inspired by the "finger pointing the moon" Buddhist koan:

> Dark night stars glitter
> The finger points the bright moon
> It is you aiming.

Writing poetry to solve problems might seem esoteric, but even *The Economist* considers it a worthy pursuit, sponsoring a contest for the best economy-related haiku.[7] Instead of confronting the problem head-on, you take a step to the side and create a desirable distance.

Distance Augments Creativity

Distance does more than offer solutions. Researchers have conducted several interesting studies on the role distance plays in augmenting creativity. For example, they were interested in how images of love and sex influence creative skills.[8] Subjects of one of the studies were asked to imagine a long walk with someone they love. Others were asked to imagine casual sex with someone attractive, though not loved. The third (control) group was asked to imagine a nice walk alone. Then all of the subjects were asked to complete tests, some of which required conventional analytic (convergent) thinking, others creative insights (divergent thinking).

The results were striking. The best at solving tasks that required creativity were those who'd imagined walking with the loved one. Whereas those asked to imagine casual sex performed poorest. With the analytic tasks, it was the reverse: those imagining lustful encounters performed best; whereas those imagining love had the lowest scores.

What do those results actually indicate? When in love, people usually take a long-term perspective, which should enhance creative thinking. Thoughts of casual sexual encounters are inherently focused on concrete details in the present and so support analytic thinking. Presumably it is distance that makes the difference.

In seems that the factor of time functions similarly. Construal Level Theory indicates that the greater the temporal distance, the more likely events will be perceived in a more abstract and general way, focused on

---

[7] See www.economist.com/blogs/freeexchange/2011/10/poetry (retrieved March 16, 2019).
[8] Förster et al. (2009); see also Kaufman (2009).

the essence and detached from the current contextual details.[9] Researchers looking at whether perceived distance in time could enable a more creative approach to problem-solving conducted a study in which subjects were told to imagine their lives in the future. One group was asked to envision a very near future, such as tomorrow, and the other, a distant future, perhaps a year from now. They were given a task and asked to imagine that they were performing it on the indicated day in the future (tomorrow or a year after). The results showed that those imagining a year in the distant future performed tasks requiring creativity better than those focused on the near future. In a series of similar experiments researchers confirmed that the distant-future perspective facilitates better abstract thinking and creative problem-solving.[10]

And what about spatial distance? Researchers explored how imagining that something was happening far away helps in creative problem-solving.[11] Subjects were told that a friendly academic team needed some support in their research. Participants were randomly divided into three groups, and the only difference between the two experimental groups was that some subjects were told that this team was located nearby, and the others were told that the team was located far away (the third control group wasn't informed about the location). Next, all subjects heard the same story about a prisoner who wanted to escape from a tower. He found a rope, but unfortunately discovered that it was half as long as needed to reach the ground safely. He divided the rope in half, tied the two parts together, and escaped. The subjects were given one minute to answer the question: how could he have done this?

Finding the solution for this case required creative thinking, as "dividing the rope" commonly means cutting it into two pieces. To find an alternative solution the subjects needed to detach their minds from conventional thinking and realize that, instead of cutting the rope in half, the prisoner divided it by unraveling the rope lengthwise and tying the two strands together.

At this point you won't be surprised to hear that the results confirmed beyond a doubt that spatial distance augments creativity. Those subjects who envisioned the prisoner's story happening far away performed significantly better than those thinking that it was just around the corner. They also did better than the control group that had no indication of distance.

---

[9] Trope and Liberman (2010).
[10] Förster et al. (2009).
[11] Jia et al. (2009); Shapira and Liberman (2009).

These experiments, and many more, corroborate the notion that temporal and spatial distance foster more abstract thinking and enhance creativity, which when brought to bear on pressing, seemingly insurmountable problems, can yield stunning results. We simply see a more panoptical picture in which the impossible may be perceived as possible.

Consultants, therapists, and experts know that there are many ways to detach our minds from current conundrums, step back and view them from a distance. Haiku writing is one. We'll look at others in the chapters that follow and give you a full array of techniques for nurturing your own possibilitivity.

Summary and Tips

> Laughter is the closest distance between two people. (Victor Borge)

The more urgent your problems are, the more you may tend to be totally preoccupied and determined to confront them, and the less creative you may be about possible solutions.

Exploring how some social entrepreneurs build peace in their region, I found that instead of confronting the conflict (as conventional conflict resolution experts do), they work to circumvent it by building alternative opportunities, such as collective small business ventures.[12]

Try avoiding an attitude of confrontation and, instead, stop thinking about the problem. Go do something else – a fun project or exercise, anything to get your mind off the issue. Then, when you're relaxed and free of stress – when you've created distance – return to thinking about a solution. Everybody should find his or her own path for this. A friend, for example, tells me that reading fairy tales to his children often gives him a new way of looking at something, and solutions he hadn't envisioned before. In my case, small talks over lunch work not only to recharge my batteries, but also are often inspirational. Also, during my morning swims, I often get invaluable "a-ha" moments. Any way of being somewhere else or in some other reality can work, especially reframing the problem and its context as a metaphor, which we'll explore next.

---

[12] See Praszkier et al. (2010).

CHAPTER 20

The Opening Value of Allegories, Metaphors, and Paradoxes

> The greatest thing by far is to be a master of metaphor; it is the one thing that cannot be learnt from others; and it is also a sign of genius, since a good metaphor implies an intuitive perception of the similarity in the dissimilar. (Aristotle)

> Metaphors have a way of holding the most truth in the least space. (Orson Scott Card, American sci-fi novelist)

So, distance helps. And, as Aristotle was perhaps the first to discover, one of the many ways to create distance is to transform the problem and its context into an allegory or metaphor – a short sentence or a longer story representing the problem in a different reality.

We use metaphors all the time and often don't even realize it. We might say that America is a melting pot or that time is money. We might call someone an early bird or sow the seeds of a new idea. In a full-blown crisis we might try to simply keep our head above water; in conflict we might try to build bridges. In each case the metaphor is the vivid association or image that represents the idea we want to convey. Some see metaphors as a "liberating force" providing new perspectives[1] and suggest that each situation or problem should be "metaphorized."[2] I share this opinion, and in my work I frequently use anecdotes and storytelling to grasp and convey the essence of a problem.

Storytelling

As more elaborate forms of metaphors, stories and anecdotes serve as allegories, in which the essential message is conveyed between the lines of the tale. These stories are ubiquitous, and we're conditioned to discern their

[1] Inkson (2002).
[2] McFadzean (1998).

meanings from a young age. The fairy tales we're told as children wrap important messages in an imagined reality.

I frequently use anecdotes when I encounter people stuck in a pattern of dysfunction. For example, when working with a team where one member held a stubborn grudge against someone else in the organization, I told this story:

> Two young Zen students were walking to their monastery. On their way they encountered a beautiful young lady whose path was blocked by a large mud puddle. One of the students picked her up and carried her across the mud. After doing so the students continued their journey.
>
> After a long time the other student said: "How could you take a woman in your hands? She is impure and must have induced you with impure thoughts!" The first student replied: "I carried her only over the mud. You are carrying her all this time."

The reaction from the individual was immediate: surprise, reflection, and laughter, followed by an insightful admission: "Indeed, I've held my grudge far too long and should have let it go a long time ago. I'll go and grab a coffee with the guy right away."

In another case, I worked with a team that couldn't make a decision without consulting an expert. Instead of trusting their judgment and taking risks, they were always pushing to hire more experts. Hence, there was no innovation, and the company was losing market share. I first tried to explain that many studies showed that experts inhibit progress, because people who consider experts more capable than themselves become less self-reliant and less proactive. But rational arguments didn't help, so I told this story:

> A Zen student graduated and was preparing to leave his monastery in the Himalayan Mountains to take a trip to the United States, where he planned to start a life on his own. Saying goodbye to his master, he asked for a cue for the independent life he was about to begin. The master said, "OK, here you are: life is like a fountain."
>
> On his way to the United States, the Zen alumni kept thinking about his master's words and wondering what "life is like a fountain" could possibly mean. He continued to ponder this for years, as he started a successful business, married and had children, and became a respected member of his community. He tried to live according to his master's recommendation, though he still couldn't grasp the essence.
>
> After many years he heard that the master was about to pass away. Immediately he went to Nepal to say goodbye to the dying man. Reaching the monastery, he spent time by the master's bed. Eventually he asked his

key question. "Dear master, all this time I've tried to understand what 'life is like a fountain' actually means; and I tried to live according to that. Could you please explain the meaning of your recommendation?" The master lifted his head and said, "Well, maybe life isn't like a fountain?"

From the group there was silence, then laughter, and then a heated discussion about the value of self-reliance. Ultimately, they realized that they had ample skills and resources and needed no help from outside experts to reach their goals.

A third example relates to individual coaching. A manager I worked with considered himself limited by personal shortcomings and was determined to change himself for the better. Consumed with the idea of improving various aspects of his personality, he signed up for courses and seminars, but was never satisfied with the results. After several sessions with him, I told him this story:

> There once was a very poor Jew named Moshe, who thought that his face was ugly and, hence, dreamed of having plastic surgery. He saved money regularly during his life and, after many years, he finally collected the sum required and went for the plastic surgery he so desired. After the operation he uncovered his face and was amazed to see how gorgeous it was.
>
> Joyfully leaving the hospital he made an unfortunate step into the street and was hit by a car. In Heaven he met God and asked, "Oh Yahweh, why did you do this to me? I waited to have a changed face for all my life and finally got it!" God responded, "Moshe, I'm sorry, but I simply didn't recognize you."

The man looked a bit stunned and then laughed. He finally understood what I meant when I encouraged him to "postpone the pursuit to be someone else." And indeed, during the following meetings he always returned to the anecdote, focusing more on his strengths and potential than on what should be changed.

Baker-Baker Paradox

Those who've heard these stories have described them as "invading and revolutionizing consciousness," sticking with people and durably influencing mindsets. This is the role of allegories, which, to use a metaphor, become sort of "mental implants" in people's minds.

Not only do allegories quickly and vividly reveal the essence of their meaning, they also function on a deeper level, engaging neuro-associations. For example, the "Baker-baker paradox" has shown that it is much easier to memorize people by their profession than by their name. In experiments, subjects viewed photographs of several people, some tagged with the individual's last name, such as Baker or Farmer, and some by their profession, such as baker or farmer. It was documented in a number of trials that recollection of the proper names was significantly poorer. The headshots were significantly more often recognized when associated with the profession.[3] This is because the name of an occupation automatically and unconsciously activates a number of associations in our memory related to the profession, whereas the individuals' names usually don't activate any associated memory circuits, unless you happen to know someone with the same name.

Furthermore, in another neuroscience experiment where subjects were asked to complete sentences using either synonyms or metaphors, it was found that creating metaphors activates parts of brain involving flexible imagination, and as a result, the construction of novel figures of speech facilitates creativity.[4]

Along these lines, the role of metaphors or allegories seems unquestionable. By presenting new concepts, metaphors "hook" the mind, building associations to important memories and thus anchoring the new concept. In that way metaphors are one of the best ways to open the mind to new ideas of what is possible.

Metaphors Used in Business

Who hasn't heard the "cathedral and the bazaar" metaphor? In the world of software design, companies like Microsoft offering software without the source code are depicted as being cathedrals built by cloistered teams of developers under the authority of a bishop, while open-source software (such as Linux) is seen as an open bazaar.[5]

Warfare metaphors are also common. Businesspeople depict companies as armies, and competition is described as a price war or territorial loss of market share.[6] Different competitive strategies are also characterized using the "red ocean" metaphor to suggest combat with competitors over limited opportunities and its opposite, the "blue ocean" metaphor, which represents a strategy to make competitors irrelevant by creating one's own "blue oceans" of uncontested market space, using one's own values and approach regardless of what competitors do.[7]

---

[3] McWeeny et al. (1987); James (2004).
[4] Benedek et al. (2014).
[5] See Raymond (2001).
[6] Talbot (2003).
[7] Kim and Mauborgne (2005).

Quite popular in business coaching are sailing metaphors: a sailboat captain who ignores changing conditions will lose the race, while a good sailboat captain watches the water's currents, the clouds, and the direction of the wind, and when conditions change, reacts accordingly.[8] Fire is another powerful metaphor for motivational forces, e.g., "burning platform" and "burning ambition."[9]

Marketing is largely based on metaphors. Marketers may depict their work as the vessel that ferries the client from an island where conditions are challenging to another where comforts abound and problems are solved.[10] Marketing slogans and taglines are also laden with colorful metaphors: Candy manufacturers invite you to taste the rainbow, and one clever soap maker promised "It's not love; it's dove."[11]

Metaphors, by definition, imply divergent thinking. They are comparisons that show how two things that are not alike in most ways are similar in another important way.[12] Metaphors play the role of a "liberating force" by providing new perspectives.[13]

One form of metaphor is paradox. Whereas metaphors or allegories may be conveyed in long stories with an eye-catching punchline, whereas paradoxes are boiled down to a simple and surprising contradiction. Paradoxes stimulate the brain's flexibility, creating more neural connections and opening up the mind to receive something new (Chapter 13).

Paradoxes in Psychotherapy

A good example of the power of paradox is its role in psychotherapy. Consider these two compelling examples.[14]

Two parents complained about their teenage son's behavior. He was hanging out with disreputable friends, didn't perform well at school, and, most disturbingly, wouldn't communicate with his parents. He simply refused to talk to them, especially when they tried to address his behavior. The parents reported this situation to the counselor but disagreed with his recommendations, claiming that they had already tried them and failed.

---

[8] See www.bizcoachinfo.com/archives/tag/sailing-business-metaphor (retrieved March 16, 2019).

[9] Fuda (2016).

[10] See http://marketingforhippies.com/metaphors-in-marketing-the-power-of-uncovering-your-core-metaphor (retrieved March 16, 2019).

[11] See www.paperlessproposal.com/how-to-use-the-power-of-metaphors-to-improve-your-sales-and-marketing (retrieved March 16, 2019).

[12] Lakoff and Johnson (2003).

[13] Inkson (2002).

[14] The first based on Wilk (1985), the second from my own experience as a family therapist.

Their weariness and helplessness were unequivocal. Given the parents' frustration, the therapist suggested that maybe more extraordinary measures were in order. He suggested that, after the son returned home and fell asleep, the parents should put his underwear in the freezer. The next morning, when the son couldn't find his briefs, he yelled at his parents, demanding to know where they were. His parents placidly replied, "In the freezer, of course."

The son went to the freezer and, in disbelief, removed his stiff and frozen briefs. Why, he asked angrily, had they put his underwear in the freezer? This triggered a series of questions and explanations, going deeper into a discussion about behavior and family communication. The confused son initiated the discussion, returning several times to the question, "OK, but why the freezer?"

The admittedly bizarre intervention reversed the family's (non-)communication pattern and created a U-turn. The paradox was that the son, who previously refused to communicate, was jolted by the sight of his underwear in the freezer, and now insisted on opening up communication in order to understand his parents' motives. And the parents, whose earlier attempts to discuss their son's behavior had failed, were now invited to get things off their chest. The family was able to resolve its problems with lightness and humor. A new "memory implant" was stored in the son's mind and, as a consequence, in the family relationship, where open communication became the new normal.

The second example comes from my own experience. A young woman told me that she had just married and that she and her new husband loved each other and everything was going well, with one exception: she loved dancing and her husband preferred reading books. Whenever there was an opportunity to go to a dance party, her husband found an excuse to stay home, and that frustrated her.

The interview and analysis didn't indicate any deeper psychological reasons for the conflict; they simply differed in terms of what they considered an evening of fun. Still, if not addressed, this seemingly insignificant difference of opinion could become a bigger problem.

I wondered what I, as a counselor, could do. Should I sit them down together for a marital counseling session and discuss this issue? That probably wouldn't help, given that they talked about the issue openly every time it came up. No, what I opted for was a paradoxical assignment, a technique often used in the family-system therapy approach.

I suggested that the next time there was an opportunity to go dancing, the woman should tell her husband that he was welcome to read while they danced. He could place his arms around her and hold his book at her back, so that while they danced, he could enjoy his book. Similarly, she would hold a book at his back, and they would dance and read together. To help her see how this could work, we played a little psychodrama, with both of us dancing while peeking at our books held behind the back of the other.

She found the whole idea funny and took it home to share with her husband. At the next session she reported that, at home, they laughed together whenever they talked about this weird counselor's suggestion. All the tension related to the original conflict disappeared, and in its place was something humorous they could share.

How did that paradoxical assignment work? I think that prior to her visit the expectation of conflict around dancing vs. reading became a cognitive pattern, more dangerous than the real situation itself. Of course I didn't expect them to actually complete the "assignment." Rather, I addressed their awareness, offering an "imagination implant" associated with the conflict and activated whenever it came up. By addressing their perception, I turned a heavy problem with potential to damage the relationship into a shared, light-hearted experience free of conflict.

Paradoxes in Operation

These examples illustrate how paradoxes can work as perception and imagination wedges, becoming sources of new cognition and inspiration. The 1960 Nobel Prize winner, Peter Medawar,[15] said that paradoxes have the same effect on a scientist or philosopher as the smell of burning rubber on an engineer: they create an irresistible urge to find the cause.

I've found paradoxes very helpful in conveying some insights that were difficult to comprehend. For example, when dealing with someone who took himself too seriously, I've commented, "A person who doesn't know how to laugh at himself is simply unserious."

While talking about the unpredictability of complex systems, I've used Samuel Goldwin's memorable quote, "Never make predictions, especially when they concern the future."

While discussing a new and risky solution I found very compelling, I've quoted Oscar Wilde: "I can resist everything but temptation."

Another Oscar Wilde paradox came in handy when highlighting a certain boss's management style: "Our boss expects you to accomplish great things, though he stops you from getting there."

---

[15] 1960 Nobel Prize winner for the discovery of acquired immunological tolerance.

And in discussions of how theory relates to practice, I've cited Yogi Berra: "In theory there is no difference between theory and practice. In practice there is."

A paradox can serve as a magnifying glass, to "enlarge" or call out an essential issue. It can also be used as an icebreaker or interlude, stimulating creative thinking and enhancing our ability to perceive by creating distance from the issue. I invite you to create your own paradoxes. Here are a few more examples – classics that might come in handy:

From Samuel Goldwyn:

> Color TV? I won't believe it until I see it in black & white.
>
> Good old days aren't what they used to be.
>
> Nobody comes here anymore – it's too crowded!
>
> I never put on a pair of shoes until I've worn them at least five years.

And from Yogi Berra:

> I never said most of the things I said.
>
> You better cut the pizza in four pieces because I'm not hungry enough to eat six.
>
> You wouldn't have won if we'd beaten you.

Summary and Tips

> The only thing you sometimes have control over is perspective. You don't have control over your situation. But you have a choice about how you view it. (Chris Pine, American actor)

Chris Pine is right. Perspective does indeed enable our control of images, cognition, and mindsets. In the case of dancing vs. reading, what changed was the couple's perspective. They learned to see the situation from a distance, adding humor and fun to it. Often gaining a new perspective is the only chance to change, as our limits are mostly controlled by our mindsets. And, by the way, this relates not only to cognitive limits, but also to physical limitations, as we'll see later.

One way to gain new perspective is through the use of allegories, metaphors, and paradoxes. They transfer the situation to a distant place and a different milieu. Distance, as we know, augments creativity and allows us to see novel solutions. We've also seen that anecdotes can help us get rid of lingering aversions or find new resources through self-reliance. And short paradoxes jolt us out of established patterns and illuminate new cognitive pathways.

These tools open the mind to the new and to perceiving new challenges as being doable, especially when our belief in "undoability" is controlled by rigid patterns of cognition. You may want to collect short inspirational stories to serve as good illustrations applicable to various situations. Stories from your own life might work perfectly, and as we saw with the Google Aristotle project, sharing personal stories also boosts creativity.

Here's an example of a story I found very inspirational for teams that were stuck and felt helpless:

> At one point during the Spanish Civil War, General Franco's troops were driving a group of two thousand Republicans into the hills near Córdoba, to a monastery they had turned into a fortress. The Republicans endured a long, hard siege that lasted for months. As long as airplanes dropped food, ammunition and medicine into the monastery, they were okay. But a shortage of parachutes threatened this supply lifeline.

The situation seemed hopeless, and the Republicans' despair didn't bring change. Then, a pilot had a crazy idea, probably conceived while hanging out in the evening with friends. He suggested something unacceptable in normal conditions, though pragmatic in wartime, that they attach the supplies to live turkeys. The turkeys flapping their wings would slow down the descent of the packages and, after delivery, the birds would provide a supply of fresh meat. Historical accounts indicate that the idea worked, and the group was able to fend off the enemy until more Republican troops came to the rescue.[16]

---

[16] From www.innovationinpractice.com/innovation_in_practice/2015/03/contradictions-a-pathway-to-creativity.html (retrieved March 16, 2019).

CHAPTER 21

Games and Simulations

I believe that simulations are a natural part of human life. Look at small children. They frequently pretend to be various characters: a train conductor, a doctor, a postman. I've observed my grandson playing a policeman and issuing fake tickets for any bit of trash on the streets, then morphing into a construction worker, whom we found hard at work excavating a hole in the hallway wall. After a visit from the plumber, he took up that line of work, which resulted in a flooded bathroom.

Such role playing is an intrinsic tendency, naturally embedded in the process of human development. It helps develop cognitive, imaginative, creative, emotional, and social spheres. Children in particular initiate these impromptu games, having an instinctual impulse to explore and experiment.

So what happens to this beautiful inclination to role play as we mature? Why, when we become adults, do we perceive such simulations as weird, unnatural, and embarrassing, participating only when required as part of some therapeutic or professional exercise? What if, instead, we tapped role playing as a tool for learning, just as we did instinctively as children, and used it to help tackle problems, unknowns, and challenges? What a great opportunity to explore areas beyond direct cognition and expand our potential for possibilitivity.

Consider these live and virtual role-playing options as places to start.

Simulation Games Online

Simulation games, also called tycoon games, enable business-skill training in a secure and virtual environment.[1] A seemingly endless array of these games give players the opportunity to found a startup,[2] manage an amusement

---

[1] Faria (1998); Seethamraju (2011).
[2] E.g., http://thefounder.biz (retrieved March 16, 2019).

park,[3] operate a farm,[4] prepare for a job,[5] or engage in some other business activity. A good sandbox for experimenting with project development is the well-known SimCity™.[6] While these games can be fun, they're also teaching tools increasingly finding their way into academic settings, where they're having a significant impact on how students prepare for the future.

Real-Life Role Playing in Business

This quote perfectly sums up real-life role playing: "Role playing is an active learning technique in which employees act out situations under the guidance of a trainer. In each scenario, employees take on a role and act out the scene as though it was real. For example, two people might simulate a meeting between an employee and an angry customer. The trainer and the other participants can then give feedback to the role players."[7]

Role playing reflects reality and, in that way, prepares participants to handle real-life situations much better than studying manuals or watching PowerPoint presentations would. It's particularly effective because it involves active group learning.

In the first phase of a role-playing exercise, participants act out a scenario with the guidance of a facilitator. By taking on various characters, participants can gain a new perspective and a deeper understanding of a situation. Then, in the second phase, the facilitator and observers in the group give feedback, which enables the participants to see their actions, behavior, body language, etc., through the eyes of others.

Role playing can be useful in a professional or academic setting and is particularly effective with younger children, who are typically comfortable pretending to be someone or something else. Role play stimulates children's imagination and empathy for the others. And as we'll see, it's also useful as a way to help children to cope with difficult situations and experiences.

Problem Solving

Most of the problems we experience in life and work can be envisioned as a drama and explored through role playing. A role-playing scenario should

---

[3] E.g., www.planetcoaster.com/en-gb (retrieved March 16, 2019).
[4] E.g., www.farming-simulator.com (retrieved March 16, 2019).
[5] E.g., https://jobsimulatorgame.com (retrieved March 16, 2019).
[6] See http://store.steampowered.com/app/24780/SimCity_4_Deluxe_Edition/ (retrieved March 16, 2019).
[7] Fuller (2018).

capture a specific issue but also leave room for an impromptu development of further action. Participants should explore a variety of scenarios, playing out different interactions and implications, followed by a round-table discussion.

For example, let's imagine a typical workplace conflict between employees handling orders from subcontractors. Ann is a fast worker and always ahead of schedule, while John is slow, usually delivering his work at the last minute. Ann does a lot of jogging, spends weekends enjoying outdoor activities, and is an extrovert. John participates in yoga courses, eats vegan food, and is a quiet introvert. At work they're often interdependent; in many cases, Ann has to wait for John to process documents, and John waits for the results of Ann's negotiations with subcontractors. This means they often run afoul of each other. Colleagues noticing the conflict discuss among themselves the hopelessness of the situation and suggest that the only solution might be to separate them.

But both Ann and John are valuable doers, so it seems worth the effort to try to resolve the conflict in their work styles. So how would we do this using role playing? First, we need to create a good scenario. One idea could be to simply replay some real-life situations. However, I wouldn't recommend this, as carbon-copying real life also transfers the feelings and mental associations associated with those situations. Instead, knowing that distance helps in finding creative solutions, I would suggest taking the key players somewhere else in time and/or space. Why not pretend to go on an expedition to a rainforest? Or open a branch of the company on a new planet? A scenario that explores a new concept will work best. In this case, we'll try this one:

The company has launched a new Corporate Social Responsibility project aimed at encouraging children to read more, instead of obsessively checking and playing with their smartphones. Staff members are sent to develop and implement this project in various regions of the country. Ann and John are delegated to go to Jefferson County in West Virginia.

The conference room is rearranged to give Ann and John their own corner for playing the simulation, while their colleagues sit at a distance, silently observing the action.

Ann talks about how important reading is for children, especially in low-income areas, where most kids have few books, if any. She mentions the example of First Book Foundation,[8] which distributes free books through

---

[8] See https://firstbook.org (retrieved March 16, 2019).

a book bank, and reaches more than three million children and educators a year, instilling a culture of reading.

Ann's body language conveys full focus and readiness for action, whereas John stays quiet, sitting in a relaxed position. This makes Ann upset. She stops talking and, after staring at John for a while, asks what he thinks about the foundation's work. John replies that he's familiar with several reading initiatives, but he's more concerned with how you make reading sufficiently attractive to compel a kid to give up time with his smartphone.

Ann reacts vigorously, "OK, but what will we achieve from sitting and thinking instead of discussing the problem?" John replies that Ann tends to speed things up, leaving no space for reflection, and Ann says that the best reflections come through sharing ideas, not through isolating oneself, and that she would appreciate knowing John's thoughts.

John replies that, yes, he has heard about First Book and its founding CEO, Kyle Zimmer. Moreover, he's read several interviews with her; in one of them Kyle Zimmer said that the children who read are playful at work, and that this playfulness makes their foundation a very creative place.[9] This makes John think that the real incentive for kids to read should be joy and play.

The discussion shifts from addressing the goal (children reading) to building a magnetic ambience. What would attract children and youth? They sit silently. Ann clearly slows down, and then John becomes visibly more energized, walking around the table. At some point Ann says that there is a need for a "magical" place. John adds, "sort of a Reading Hogwarts?" Do we know such a place?

Their colleagues see that something had changed in the quality of their interaction. Ann and John cooperatively share their ideas through a process of communication that includes both silence and reflection and a more energized back-and-forth of ideas. A smooth exchange replaces earlier frustration.

At some point John has an a-ha moment. What if the "magical place" in Jefferson County was Harpers Ferry, a historical location situated on a hilltop in Maryland Heights, with a gorgeous view of forests, valleys, and the junction of Shenandoah and Potomac rivers? (See Figure 13.)

John has been there recently, while trekking the Appalachian Trail and meditating, and found the famous historical Hill Top Hotel, built in 1888, but vacant and deteriorating since 2008. Ann looks the place up on Google

---

[9] See www.nytimes.com/2012/05/27/business/first-books-kyle-zimmer-on-rewarding-good-ideas-that-fail.html (retrieved March 16, 2019).

Figure 13 Historic Harpers Ferry at the junction of the Shenandoah and Potomac rivers.
Photos: Ryszard Praszkier.

and finds that it has hosted such luminaries as Alexander Graham Bell, Mark Twain, and President Bill Clinton. She also learns that Harpers Ferry is well known for the abolitionist John Brown's 1859 raid on an armory, which was a harbinger of the Civil War.

John is at that point again sitting relaxed, and Ann is pacing back and forth. However, now their conversation is easy and light. When Ann says with humor that John has once again gone mute and motionless, John replies with a smile that Ann is once again a ball of energy. They both laugh, acknowledging that a little humor and fun can lead to new ideas.

And the ideas keep coming. They decide to rent what remains of the Hill Top Hotel and build a book maze where kids can search for books on the history of the region, clustered according to age. They'll dig for information and play the role of "miners" exploring the mines of knowledge. This could include tours of nearby historical sites, such as the remains of the original fort seized by John Brown, and trips to the hills on the opposite side of Hill Top. Finally, kids could participate in a contest, reporting the results of their "information search and mining" and reading aloud from the books they found. Needless to say, all smartphones would be collected at the beginning of the visit, so the kids would have to turn to books for information.

Ann and John's role playing concludes with an action plan for a feasibility study to look at options for renting the abandoned hotel and raising funds for reconstruction and renovation. They're sure that the prospect of a grand tourist attraction will motivate collaboration, and that the First Book Foundation will supply the books. It seems they can't stop generating ideas, and their communication and mutual understanding is immensely improved.

At the end of the session, the observers share their feedback. The most important comments relate to how Ann and John's workstyle differences complement rather than conflict with the other's, and how they make an ideal team, with John's reflection-centered and Ann's action-oriented attitude. They all feel sure that the role-playing experience will set Ann and John on a new, more positive and collaborative path.

Family Role Playing

Simulations through role playing can also be used in a family setting. Scenarios might relate to specific problems or simply explore options. For example, two young siblings could act out hitting their neighbor's window while playing softball, and then discuss what to do next. Or a father and his 16-year-old daughter could simulate driving lessons using the father's precious car. Or a 16-year-old boy could pretend to be at his first interview for a part-time job at a local store.[10]

If we want to explore situations more remote in space and time (because we know that distance helps), we might pretend our family is on a desert island or an alien planet. This can be a lot of fun and also provide an opportunity to circumvent natural constraints that can pop up when mirroring real life.

Role Playing: Expanding Possibilitivity

Role playing engages both the key actors and the observing team (or rest of the family). If the scenario is significantly different from the real-life problems it seeks to solve (though reflects those problems in the new context), then participants can shed habitual reactions and attributions more easily and be open to experience greater empathetic understanding of the others.

In other words, role playing offers an out-of-the-box journey. It trains the mind to become free from rigid behavior and cognitive patterns, opening a new, free space for exploring what previously seemed impossible. In our example of Ann and John, the prevailing belief was that they wouldn't be able to work together. But seeing how seemingly unsolvable conflicts can be harnessed into efficient cooperation helps participants see the potential for similar solutions in the future. They become equipped with a generalized cognition that *it is possible to turn Impossible to Possible.*

Summary and Tips

Role playing is a natural, spontaneous propensity in childhood. Later in life, we become more "serious" and lose this ability. Then we try to fill the gap with more artificial methods, such as using online simulations. These can be useful for training purposes, but I encourage you to try live role-playing scenarios to solve problems at work, in school, or with family.

Use your imagination to develop scenarios far removed from the situation you want to address, understanding that creative role playing can help us be more empathetic toward others and more open to exploring new options, making bold decisions, and seeing undiscovered possibilities. Using role playing may be one of the best ways to remove the mind's barriers and to see the undoable as possible.

---

[10] Examples from www.lds.org/manual/family-home-evening-resource-book/family-activities/role-playing?lang=eng (retrieved March 16, 2019).

CHAPTER 22

Joy and Dancing
A Royal Way to Opening the Mind

> The creation of something new is not accomplished by the intellect
> but by the play instinct. (Carl Jung)
>
> If you want creative workers, give them enough time to play. (John
> Cleese)
>
> He laughed to free himself from his mind's bondage. (James Joyce)

My close friend, a successful North American businessman, likes to tell me
that I don't know business. That all this writing about joy, role playing, and
dancing has nothing to do with how the real business world works. Real
business means diligent market analysis, low- and high-level planning,
putting a business plan on paper, he tells me. My reply? I agree. All of
that is critical to business success. But if you want to raise the bar and take
things to the next level, you need something more. And the "more" is creativity and the ability to see as doable things that others see as undoable.
To make my point, I shared with him the following story:

At the end of 1994, I was hired as an Ashoka representative for Poland.[1]
Ashoka is a global association in operation since 1980, and currently in
more than 80 countries. Its mission was to find, select, and empower
social entrepreneurs who find novel solutions to pressing, though seemingly insurmountable, social problems and implement systemic change in
the field.

My task was to identify these special individuals as candidates for
the Ashoka Fellowship. I took it very seriously, learning about the concept of social entrepreneurship, which at that time wasn't known in
Poland, and searching for candidates, often in the most remote areas.
I was convinced they were out there, in some cases living in underprivil-
eged rural areas, having little formal education and knowing nothing of
Ashoka or our grant program. (The internet was in its nascent stages at

---

[1] See www.ashoka.org (retrieved March 16, 2019).

this point.) In fact, stories about my search for Ashoka candidates could fill another book.[2]

Once the first cohorts of Ashoka Fellows were elected, my next passion was to build a strong community, so the Fellows would feel bonded, provide mutual support to one another, work together on new off-shoot ideas, and create an environment where they could recharge their personal batteries. At that time there was no widely accepted research or knowledge on social capital and the power of horizontal networks. All that I had to go on was my instinct.

Following a hunch, I added to the agenda of official meetings a series of off-the-record gatherings, with round-table discussion. I wanted Ashoka Fellows to take co-ownership of their time together and come up with their own ideas. It worked. The informal, impromptu meetings generated valuable and sometimes heated discussions, and a number of new ideas the Fellows were eager to pursue on their own. One of those ideas was the Ashoka School of Young Social Entrepreneurs (ASYSE), where Ashoka Fellows met with university students, shared their experiences, and invited them to apply for internships.[3] This initiative spread to Nepal and Indonesia, operated for several years, and led to the establishment of a vital ASYSE alumni network that is still active today.

I firmly believe that these bottom-up initiatives wouldn't have happened if the Fellows' interactions had been limited to formal meetings. By giving them the opportunity to loosen up a bit, joke, and have fun, we facilitated not only their camaraderie and spontaneous and innovative thinking, but also their propensity for sharing and probing new initiatives.

Needless to say, not everyone in the Ashoka organization understood and appreciated this sort of approach. I remember one of the executive-team members mocking us by labeling these kinds of meetings as "happy-happy." This person was convinced that the organization needed only intense concentration on goals, without the distractions of social engagement and unstructured communication.

I wasn't aware at the time that studies, which had already started in the early 1990s and continue today, had proven her wrong. In fact, playfulness, relaxation, joy, and happiness all enhance creativity and, in that way, enhance an organization's performance.

---

[2] You may find more on that in our previous book, *Social Entrepreneurship: Theory and Practice* (Praszkier & Nowak, 2012).
[3] For more about Ashoka School for Young Social Entrepreneurs (ASYSE) see Praszkier (2018, pp. 149–152).

The Power of Joy

It was as early as the 1990s when several studies documented that a positive attitude, even if induced by simply watching a few minutes of a comedy film or receiving a small bag of candy, improves performance on many cognitive tasks,[4] especially those requiring a creative approach.[5] In the 1990s, the American psychology professor Mihály Csíkszentmihályi published his renowned book, *Creativity: Flow and the Psychology of Discovery and Invention*[6] and an article titled "Happiness and creativity."[7] In interviews with leading creatives from diverse disciplines, he asked several questions, including, "What is the secret to making activities rewarding?" The most common response was, "designing or discovering something new." The author's conclusion was that it is joy that keeps people engaged in innovation, and conversely, new ideas bring a feeling of happiness.

These early studies paved the way for much research. One study examined the diaries of 222 employees in seven companies and found that the more positive the attitude, the higher the creativity.[8] Generally, it was affirmed that a sense of humor helps to reduce stress and makes it possible to look at problems from a new perspective.[9]

Humor can also help people survive extreme oppression. Prisoners of war (POWs) have often found humor to be an effective coping mechanism, a way of fighting back and taking control. Interviews with 50 Vietnam POWs confirmed the power of humor,[10] and studies of the Holocaust revealed that humor helped Nazi victims endure extreme oppression by focusing attention on what was wrong and sparking resistance to it, creating solidarity in those who laughed at the oppressors together, and helping the oppressed get through their suffering without going insane.[11]

This was also my experience when I participated in Solidarity, the peaceful Polish underground movement of the 1980s. In spite of the curfew, the tanks on the street, and the arrests and detentions, people created their own *sub rosa* civil society, with underground publishing and illegal information sharing in private homes. Most actors boycotted the

[4] Gregory et al. (1999).
[5] Isen et al. (1987).
[6] Csíkszentmihályi (1997a).
[7] Csíkszentmihályi (1997b).
[8] Amabile et al. (2005).
[9] Caudron (1992); Abel (2002).
[10] Henman (2001).
[11] Morreal (2001).

official propagandist TV and performed illegally, circumventing censorship. All this was done with humor, shared through stories of those who had out-smarted and cheated the regime.

A favorite was one about the Orange Alternative, a group that used humor and absurdity to ridicule the regime (mentioned in Chapter 4). For example, to cleverly address the chronic shortage of toilet paper, a member of the group dressed as Santa Claus at Christmastime and handed out rolls of toilet paper for free. A huge crowd gathered in the main square, waving their toilet paper and laughing about it. The police were helpless to act because no law was broken, even though the spectacle made them look ridiculous. When the police finally did step in and arrest "Santa," the crowd chanted, "Free Santa Claus!" avoiding any direct criticism of the regime. Because the activist playing Santa hadn't done anything illegal, he was soon released. Afterwards, Santa Claus remained a symbol of resistance, and buildings were covered with drawings of his iconic cap, putting authorities in the embarrassing position of having to scrub the walls all over the town.

Such stories encouraged people to be creative in building their own, independent civil society alongside the regime, creating something of an alternative reality. It's likely that this decade-long experience contributed to the skyrocketing number of new startups just after the peaceful turnover of power in 1989.

Joy at Work

The approach that uses joy to foster performance is especially applicable to the workplace. Some psychologists promote the idea that every employee should be able to achieve joy at work and that joy leads to improved quality and a high-performance organization. Remember Ricardo Semler saying that the purpose of work is to feel good about life (Chapter 1). The research on happiness in the context of positive psychology supports this notion and finds that seeking happiness is consistent with seeking high performance.[12]

The best illustration of this is the book *Joy at Work: A Revolutionary Approach to Fun on the Job*.[13] The author, Dennis W. Bakke, tells the story of the AES Corporation, a rather atypical Fortune 500 and Forbes Global 2000 energy company whose business model and operating ethos from

[12] Miller (2013).
[13] Bakke (2006).

the beginning (when Bakke and his friend conceived the idea during a 90-minute car ride from Annapolis, MD, to Washington, DC) was "let's have fun." Since then, the partners have managed their company using a highly unusual, decentralized business model. The results? AES became a worldwide energy giant with 40,000 employees in 31 countries and annual revenues of $8.6 billion.

Bakke rejected workplace drudgery, which he describes as a noxious remnant of the Industrial Revolution. He believes work should be fun, and at AES he set out to prove that it could be. To be clear, Bakke isn't talking about the "empty fun" of Friday beers, but the joy of a workplace where every person, from custodian to CEO, has the power to use his or her talents free of corporate bureaucracy. Bakke's vision was to orchestrate a corporate mind-shift into integrity, fairness, social responsibility, and a sense of fun.[14]

Similarly, people at Morning Star,[15] the largest tomato processor in the world, call work the "Tomato Game" and can't wait for the weekend to be over so they can get back to the play of work as self-managers. This extraordinarily successful company handles nearly 40 percent of all the tomatoes processed each year in the United States, with more than 400 year-round employees and many returning seasonal workers producing more than $700 million in annual revenue. Morning Star embraces the principles of self-management: all employees, regardless of their education or position, are called colleagues. They have no bosses and no top-down control. Instead, the company urges them to find joy and excitement in working to their potential, and above all, taking personal responsibility and holding themselves accountable for achieving the company's "Big Mission," as well as their own personal missions. As a result Morning Star colleagues find the Tomato Game greatly satisfying.

Dance to Innovate

Why dance? Because no other pastime so intensively integrates emotions, empathy, kinesthetic orientation, movement neuroscience, and harmony. Dance also provides a way of learning, by developing communication abilities, problem-solving techniques, and creative and critical thinking.

---

[14] It's worth mentioning that after he retired he and his wife founded (with $155 million of the fortune Dennis Bakke had earned as CEO of AES Corporation) 55 Imagine Schools in nine states, which enrolled 29,812 students in 2015.

[15] Founded by Chris Rufer in 1970.

Figure 14 AIESEC members starting morning session with dancing.
Permission received from AIESEC.

Dance movement becomes the medium for sensing, understanding, and communicating ideas, feelings, and experiences.[16]

Before, I briefly mentioned the international youth organization AIESEC, with its dancing icebreakers held each morning at conferences. Operating since 1948, and currently in 126 countries, AIESEC unites university students in their exploration of peace and fulfillment of humankind's potential. I was invited to present at some of AIESEC's international meetings and found them to be amazing experiences. The students work intensively during the day, socialize until late at night, sharing food from their native countries, and wake up on time for their early morning session. Each morning starts with dancing. The students gather on the stage and find a common rhythm in the movement (see Figure 14). They proudly declare that "during a dance, joy and happiness bring up the best in people and differences are, for a moment, forgotten or embraced and cherished."[17]

For these students, dancing serves as a daily icebreaker and connector by stimulating kinesthetic empathy, harmony, openness to others, and

[16] Kogon (2013).
[17] See http://aiesec.no/dancing-way-world-peace/ (retrieved March 16, 2019).

creativity. And indeed, after dancing, they head right to challenging sessions, where they work on enabling cross-country cooperation to build a world of sustainable development and peace.

Business as Dancing

It's no wonder then that there are numerous analogues between business and dancing. One related book, *The Dance of Leadership: The Art of Leading in Business, Government, and Society*,[18] opens a window on how to apply the principles of dance to improve individual and organizational leadership. The premise of the book is to demonstrate that leaders, like dancers, rely on their passion, intuition, and discipline to refine their craft and connect with their clients and colleagues.

Businesspeople also need to negotiate and sync with their partners, similar to the way dancers synchronize. As one professional dancer put it, businesspeople should integrate the creative process into their work the way dancers "integrate moves into their bodies."[19] Valeh Nazemoff, who, in her words, is "a business owner by day and a competitive ballroom dancer by night," says that she discovered how much the two seemingly different domains have in common. Ballroom dance partners must be in perfect, harmonious step with each other, which can only be accomplished through ongoing communication and practice. The same is true in business.[20]

Nazemoff wrote in her book, *The Dance of the Business Mind*, that if you approach your business as a choreographer and see the relationships as a dance, then you may be much more sensitive both to the substance as well as to the context. The choreographer takes into account multiple issues, looks around corners, sees the stage elements, plans collaboration, thinks about the audience's reaction, and most importantly, envisions coordination between all elements. It may help immensely in business to use the same sensitive and harmony-based approach to planning the relationships between your colleagues, clients, marketplace, negotiations, etc.

In her book, Nazemoff focuses on the mind and how to open it up to visualizing business as dancing, and sensing the harmony of the multiplicity of elements – mission, communication, rhythm, ambience – which must be in sync.[21]

---

[18] Denhardt and Denhardt (2015).
[19] See www.inc.com/dev-aujla/what-dance-can-teach-business.html (retrieved March 16, 2019).
[20] Nazemoff (2015).
[21] Nazemoff (2017).

Dancing Keeps You Healthy

> Aging is an issue of mind over matter. If you don't mind – it doesn't matter. (Mark Twain)

In multiple studies researchers have compared the effects of several different activities on aging. They've found that frequent reading led to a 35 percent reduction in the risk of dementia, doing crossword puzzles at least four days a week reduced risk by 47 percent, and dancing reduced risk by 76 percent. So yes, frequent dancing has a magical effect on the mind and body. Dancing integrates several brain functions at once. Simultaneous kinesthetic, cognitive, musical, and emotional activity increases neuronal connectivity, which leads to greater complexity of the neuronal synapses and lower risk of cognitive decline.[22]

And those who dance frequently enjoy the way it feels, especially when they're fully engaged in alternating between spontaneous leading and empathetic following. Both leading and following benefit from a highly active attention to possibilities. Both require and support empathy, which fires groups of neurons called "mirror neurons" and exercises your brain's plasticity.[23]

Dance is also used in education as a vehicle for sensing, understanding, and communicating. As such, dance becomes an avenue for specific learning, which develops communication abilities, problem-solving techniques, and creative and critical thinking skills, along with kinesthetic abilities.[24] Moreover, dance helps people with Parkinson's disease. As academician, psychologist, and former professional dancer Peter Lovatt, Ph.D., put it, "dancing can change the way you think."[25] Those who remain skeptical may want to watch the clip of a group from New Zealand, all pushing 80, and performing a hip-hop number that won the Hip-Hop International championship in Las Vegas (2013).[26]

Dance for Empathy

Studies indicate that dancers are typically more emotionally sensitive than the rest of us.[27] One of the best examples of the power of dance is the dance

---

[22] Powers (2010); Majd (2012); Bergland (2013).
[23] Praszkier (2014).
[24] Kogon (2013).
[25] See www.theguardian.com/tedx/peter-lovatt-dance (retrieved March 16, 2019).
[26] See http://hiphoperationthemovie.com; see their photo at www.irishexaminer.com/lifestyle/healthandlife/yourhealth/ageing-with-attitude-thehip-operation-crew-move-to-the-beat-at-80-and-beyond-356775.html (both retrieved March 16, 2019).
[27] Christensen et al. (2016).

program for children in underserved areas provided by the non-profit Dancing Classrooms.[28] *The Atlantic* magazine featured the group's dancing lessons for fifth-graders at an elementary school located in one of Los Angeles's most violent neighborhoods.[29] Dancing brings them a feeling of safety and helps them synchronize with others. It's a powerful tool for teaching empathy and cooperation, and in my opinion, it should be part of every elementary school curriculum.

Dancing could also enrich business training programs, helping leaders and staff more deeply understand their partners' feelings and intentions, and how to suitably respond to them.

Finally, family dancing, be it impromptu or planned, could immensely enhance mutual understanding and deepen family relationships.

Possibilitivity

Joy, humor, and dancing have the power to enhance how you think, feel, and move. They expand your perspective on problems and challenges, making things others see as impossible, seem within reach for you. A good illustration is Lovatt talking about his life and how it changed thanks to dancing.

"In school I was rubbish and everything I have done in school was completely rubbish," he says. Dancing, it turned out, was his natural way to live and communicate. And through dancing, he gained self-esteem and ultimately became an academician.[30]

Summary and Tips

In Chapter 12, we talked about the role of brain plasticity and neurotransmitters, and how some of them, like dopamine and endorphins, also serve as joy hormones. Many scholars confirm that humor increases creativity and helps reframe our thinking as more divergent.[31]

Gloomy offices with isolated boxes devastate creativity and possibilitivity. Fortunately architects are designing new offices as open spaces, prompting divergent and accidental encounters, and providing a variety of joyful opportunities. For example, instead of a traditional staircase, Google's

---

[28] See www.dancingclassrooms.org (retrieved March 16, 2019).
[29] See www.theatlantic.com/education/archive/2016/01/learning-empathy-through-dance/426498 (retrieved March 16, 2019).
[30] Lovatt talking: www.theguardian.com/tedx/peter-lovatt-dance (retrieved March 16, 2019).
[31] McFadzean (1998); Russ (2003); Von Oech (2008); Koestler (2009); Pellis and Pellis (2009).

Engineering Hub in Zurich includes a whimsical method of access from the second floor to the first.[32]

And remember, dancing helps. Dance often and dance in a way that requires tuning into your partner's movements. Music is also important for the rhythm it prompts. Add dancing to your teambuilding activities, or start a dance competition at your work. Have fun and dance at home with your family, too.

---

[32] See www.archdaily.com/41400/google-emea-engineering-hub-camezind-evolution/5011f11128ba0d 5f4c0005c4-google-emea-engineering-hub-camezind-evolution-photo (retrieved March 16, 2019).

CHAPTER 23

A Flexible Body Opens the Mind

Mind–body dualism is one of the oldest human concepts. Coined by Plato, continued by Aristotle, and invigorated by Descartes, it's been upheld throughout the twentieth century by many philosophers.[1] However, the converse concept of mind–body unity has also gained support,[2] the most outstanding advocate for this narrative being Sondra Fraleigh, Professor Emeritus of the State University of New York, where she chaired the Department of Dance. Fraleigh makes one of the most compelling cases for this view in her book *Dance and the Lived Body*,[3] which presents dance as a state of mind–body integration.

Professor Fraleigh is also an expert in human development through bodily techniques. Her passion as a therapist centers on body awareness. In medical terms, one focus of her work is expanding *proprioception*.

The Significance of Proprioception

Proprioception is the sense of the position of parts of one's body and of the strength of effort employed in movement. In other words, it's the ability to sense one's orientation, as well as sensory awareness of movement of the body and its parts. It differs from perceiving the outside world (*exteroception*), and from sensing one's pain or hunger (*interoception*).

The famous neurologist Oliver Sacks (author of my favorite book *The Man Who Mistook His Wife For A Hat*), writes that proprioception indicates the feeling of "possessing" one's body thanks to a constant flow of incoming information from the muscles, joints, and tendons. One "owns"

---

[1] E.g., by Australian philosopher, David Chalmers, proponent of naturalistic dualism, or by Clive Staples Lewis, writer and theologian.
[2] E.g., by French phenomenological philosopher Maurice Merleau-Ponty.
[3] Fraleigh (1998).

oneself, because the body knows itself and confirms itself by this "sixth sense."[4]

What we call "body image" is actually an integration of tangible neural messages (proprioception) with vaguer sources of identity, such as advertisements, peer pressure, family influence, and fashion trends. In turn, our sense of self-esteem and level of performance comes largely from our body image.[5] Therefore, it seems exceptionally important to strengthen the "real" messages that our mind receives from our body and not be overwhelmed with indeterminable and volatile factors coming from outside of ourselves. Expanding our proprioception contributes to the authentic construction of our body image and, as a result, to our performance. This is probably why Fraleigh, aside from being a dance professor, is also a licensed Feldenkrais trainer.

Feldenkrais' Discoveries

The Feldenkrais approach uses gentle, mindful movements to expand the body's range of motion in a balanced way. Practitioners seek to achieve overall bodily harmony rather than concrete goals, as they might through regular physical training or rehabilitation.

The premise of the Feldenkrais method is that style and range of motion is controlled by the brain, so the brain (rather than the muscles) should be the focus for enhancing one's range of motion or alleviating pain caused by bad movement habits.

Movements are complex. Even simple ones, like grabbing a cup of coffee, involve coordination of neuronal impulses to dozens of muscles and tendons in the arms and fingers, stretching and releasing the tension. A baby clumsily explores new movements through trial and error, and, after mastering the movement, stores its pattern in a specific neural localization, ready to be used throughout its entire life. Those patterns are a blessing, helping us to perform complex movements in the blink of an eye, without even noticing their complexity. On the other hand, some of those templates get stored when we're in pain. These also linger, staying with us long after the pain is gone and limiting our physical abilities.

The foundation of Feldenkrais' approach is that, to expand human motoric potential, one needs to replace old templates stored in the brain with new ones, and that this can be done by building harmony, without

[4] Sacks (1998).
[5] E.g., Tallat et al. (2017).

stressful stretching or painful bending. In fact, the subtler the better. In some situations, to avoid forceful and painful actions, it's even enough to simply imagine the new set of movements.

The core practice includes a few hundred movement sets, which are new for the brain and, as such, stimulate new neuronal connections (brain plasticity) to accommodate and create templates for the new motion. These unusual and un-practiced movement challenges the brain to adapt; for example:

In the first step, you stand straight and swing your hips to the right and then to the left, without bending your body. Try to do it smoothly, not forcefully, playing with it just to the point at which it becomes stressful or painful.

In the second stage you swing your hips to the right, while turning your shoulder to the left, and then do the opposite, simultaneously and smoothly performing two contradictory movements. The third stage is to move your hips to one side, your shoulders to the other side, and turn your head to the same side as the hips. Again, play with the motion, find your best harmony and don't force it. If it's too challenging, do it only in your imagination.

In the final stage you add eye movements, looking in the opposite direction your head turns (and the same direction your shoulders move). Play with performing all four contradictory movements simultaneously. Do it not as an "exercise" aimed at achieving a result, but as a pleasant exploration and a means to enjoy your body's harmony.

The idea behind this method is that only subtle movements can facilitate the new pattern's storage in the brain, whereas stressful exercising, pulling and pushing can influence only the muscles and joints, and, in some extreme situations, may result in permanent damage. A combination of delicate and unexpected actions gently provokes the brain and becomes a way to modify stored neural patterns, expanding our ability to move.

Moshe Feldenkrais, a doctor of science (Sorbonne), was an engineer, physicist, inventor, martial artist, and student of human development. A passionate soccer player, in 1920 he "chronically" injured his knee during a game. Doctors said he would never be able to play sports again.

Undaunted, Feldenkrais decided to apply knowledge gained from his study of physics, engineering, and martial arts to an intensive self-study of his own movement habits. He was convinced his cure would come through influencing motor patterns. Studies and probes on his own body did indeed bring relief, allowing him to avoid knee surgery and return to sports. He then piloted the methods he developed on himself with a small group of people, identifying a few hundred techniques, each connected with different movement abilities. He set up workshops in many countries to share the techniques he called "functional integration" and, in 1949, wrote *Body and Mature Behavior*[6] followed by several more books.

Inspired by my results with the Feldenkrais techniques, I also piloted a workshop with a group of high-mountain climbers. They were all extremely strong and agile, though most of them suffered some spinal or joint pain as a result of their intensely physical climbing activities. After playing with two dozen Feldenkrais-inspired techniques, they reported great relief from pain and were able to strike a broader range of movements. Once they realized that it's possible to achieve the same (or better) fitness results with less exertion and strain, they transferred the same approach to their everyday lives to address other stressful challenges. The revelation that harmonious movements could release tension and bring pleasure not only improved their climbing, but also their lives in general.

There's no doubt that Feldenkrais techniques influence the level of proprioception, providing better feedback about the way we move. This, in a chain reaction, contributes to building a better body image and, as a result, to achieving more of what we want from our bodies.

Alexander Technique

The importance of having high levels of proprioception – being fully attentive to the state of all acting muscles – is also highlighted in the Alexander technique,[7] which emphasizes awareness strategies applied to action.

Frederick Matthias Alexander believed that poor movement habits damage not only health, but also proprioception. Similar to Feldenkrais, he was convinced that movement efficiency supports overall physical well-being. And, like Feldenkrais, he also saw his approach not as an exercise of muscles and joints, but as a form of mental training.

Born in the 1860s, in Australia, Alexander was an actor. He was rehearsing for a Shakespeare play when he unexpectedly lost his voice. The many professionals he visited in search of a cure recommended treatments that turned out to be useless. Especially puzzling was that he didn't lose

---

[6] Feldenkrais (2005); see also *The Potent Self* (Feldenkrais, 2002, first published in 1985).

[7] Alexander (1984, first published in 1932).

his voice with everyday speaking, yet while performing his voice became hoarse and he was unable to complete the performance.

For relief, he turned, as Feldenkrais had done, to self-investigations, resulting in what is known today as the Alexander technique. Experimenting with head and neck positioning, he discovered that some habitual positions and movements were impeding his expression and quality of voice. Through his self-experiments, he eventually regained full use of his voice. He then developed several techniques to help others overcome their own dysfunctions and use their bodies better as a whole.

The Alexander technique often focuses on sitting, standing, and lying down to find the best movements for the head position – all in the direction of lengthening the body, as we usually tend to hunch over and slouch. The pupil's focus is to lengthen while maintaining the upright central positioning of the head, neck, and spine.

A typical Alexander technique lesson involves taking a close look at the student's patterns during common movements such as bending, walking, reaching, sitting at the computer, standing, etc. The student learns to do everyday actions with less muscular tension. Part of each lesson is devoted to the teacher assisting the release of tension while the student lies on a massage table.

In Feldenkrais' workgroups, clients are guided through many different sequences that create unexpected sets of movements for the brain and increase the range of motions in the most harmonious way. The trainer defines the desired final position, but students must find their own way to achieve this end result with minimal tension, and only up to the point of pain. In that vein, they probe and play until they find the most harmonious path. If they feel incapable of performing without pain, they can opt to do the movement in their imagination, because the addressee is the brain, not the muscles.

Both the Alexander and Feldenkrais methods are educational techniques aimed at establishing a heightened proprioception. Both techniques hold that some habitual movements lead to movement problems and pain. By changing these patterns, the entire system or body functions better. These teachers believed that movement is only a secondary function of the body, the primary being the function of the mind. They also held that mind and body should not be viewed separately but as a whole, supporting the concept of mind–body unity.[8]

---

[8] Jain et al. (2004).

Figure 15 The typical Feldenkrais sitting position.
Illustration by Magdalena Hollender.

Brain Plasticity Through Body Movements and Possibilitivity

New and unexpected sets of movements, if gentle, lead to an increase of brain plasticity, as new neuronal paths have to be set up in order to accommodate the new patterns. In my personal experience, playing regularly with Feldenkrais techniques not only enhances my proprioception, supporting the efficiency of my movements, but also augments the propensity for brain plasticity in other areas, making it easier to innovate and write for example. Metaphorically, this is the way I experience Sondra Fraleigh's concept of the "Lived Body."

Together with other techniques we've mentioned (simulations, metaphors, and dancing), these methods help develop the potential for sustained neuroplasticity. In the next chapter we will mention yet another important path leading in the same direction.

Summary and Tips

Playing with body movements can be done at any time during the day. I do it in the morning, and when taking short breaks during my work time. You may also consider brief group sessions over the lunch break, rotating the facilitator's role and using different techniques. Make sure you have a secure carpet or hard exercise mattresses, as well as room for each participant to roll.

I usually start with the hips-shoulder-head-eyes technique mentioned above. Next, while lying on my back, I do the Pelvic Clock exercise (see the website),[9] and then play with lying down and transitioning to the specific Feldenkrais sitting position (see Figure 15).

Lying on my back, I start moving my head left and right, initially slowly and then more quickly. Gradually I add the shoulders, following the head's movement. Then I add hand-swinging accordingly and, at the point when I feel that the dynamics permit it, I follow my arm with my body, turning to the side in a corkscrew way and moving to sitting position.[10]

The most important thing to keep in mind is the overall influence of your body's flexibility, harmony, and balance on your mental performance, especially as it relates to opening the mind to new and challenging issues.

[9] See http://shift.nyc/2016/03/10/lessons-from-feldenkrais-part-1-the-pelvic-clock/ (retrieved March 16, 2019).
[10] You may find some more Feldenkrais guidance at www.youtube.com/watch?v=ZSletIPIN30 (retrieved March 16, 2019).

CHAPTER 24

Imagination as a Key to the Impossible

Imagination is more important than knowledge. For knowledge is limited to all we now know and understand, while imagination embraces the entire world, and all there ever will be to know and understand. (Albert Einstein)

Laughter is timeless, imagination has no age and dreams are forever. (Walt Disney)

The true sign of intelligence is not knowledge but imagination. (Albert Einstein)

Imagination is the key to a better quality of life and to your business success. Through imagination you may get into areas far from your everyday experience, far beyond your knowledge, and far from your "down to earth" realistic and practical thinking; the unexpected happens and the impossible becomes possible.[1] The following scenarios illustrate how imagination allows us to envision possibilities beyond the actualities in which we are immersed.[2]

The Tedious Family

I will always remember my "tedious family" case. The referral came because of problems with Caty, who, at the age of 16, was at risk of developing a serious eating disorder. She hadn't yet reached a state of dangerous anorexia, but she was moving in that direction. Her younger brother, Alex, 14, was an energetic lad, involved in sports and seemingly not much interested in family matters. Both parents were committed to doing something about Caty's problem. And after a series of individual interviews with family members, they agreed to have a few family sessions.

---

[1] See Faucette (2012).
[2] Hanson (1988).

The sessions went well; we discussed everyday issues and reasons why Caty avoided eating. Her avoidance seemed tied to her school friends and their preoccupation with studying and trying new diet schemes. However, at some point I had the feeling that we were stuck; Caty had started to eat normally, but communication in the family was still only on the surface, not reaching emotions, either positive or negative. There were no vibrant exchanges, no surprises, no unexpected flowers given; they basically remained correct and formal. I realized that this was simply how this family operated – reserved and predictable.

That's why my private moniker for them was "the tedious family." Everyone needs some outstanding events in life, whether it's unexpected tickets to the theater or an exciting trip, or a surprise on a day that isn't Mother's Day or a birthday – anything to break the routine. It seemed that without these unplanned moments, the family's underlying emotions – positive and negative – simply had no way to be vented, and so were kept suppressed.

This situation became a real problem, so I discussed it with my colleagues. Everybody agreed that, on the one hand, as Caty's problem was resolved, we could conclude therapy. But on the other, given how the family functioned, a relapse was likely. These suppressed issues probably contributed to Caty's eating disorder, which was an indirect call for attention. The challenge was how to make a dull family come alive. Nobody seemed to have solution. So I turned to guided imagination, a technique I used as a possible means to address seemingly insurmountable problems.

During a session, I asked the family members to close their eyes and imagine that the person sitting on their left side was doing something stupid. A heavy silence hung in the air, and then Alex started giggling. After a while so did the mother, followed by Caty and the father. When Alex finally burst into laughter, I asked them to open their eyes and share what they had imagined.

Alex couldn't wait, recounting that he imagined his father pouring noodles on his own head, an image he found hilarious. They all vigorously shared what they had imagined, laughing and commenting how funny the images were. This is how they left the session and, surprisingly, how they started the next meeting. Apparently, the notion of noodles on Dad's head was the hit of the week, during which they had organized outdoor activities and planned to go to a baseball game together. At the next session and the few that followed, the family reached a new level of communication, embracing a full range of emotions and sharing their true thoughts with one another.

The power of imagination turned out to be both a short-term fix, providing a means to release suppressed tension and emotions, and a long-term solution, as the new images became a shared experience they frequently referred to. I wondered if what I had done was to set some solid "imagination implants" in their minds.

Revival of the Wall Clocks

Let's imagine that we've been asked to provide consultation for a wall clock company with long traditions, currently facing a declining market and formidable competitors. The company has tried hard to hold on, but the ubiquitous presence of smartphones and household devices with electronic clocks has crippled market demand. On top of that, competitors are offering new designs addressed to the specific market segments, like Transformers for kids and Star Wars for teens. The company is facing downfall and bankruptcy.

After a series of initial interviews to assess the problem, we call a staff meeting to explore future trends. By suggesting that this will be an opportunity to play with options rather than a doom-and-gloom assessment, we get a positive response from the start.

We start with some ice-breaking anecdotes, like the one about a chemist, physicist, and computer engineer riding in a car, which suddenly stops. The chemist suggests that something must have changed the chemical composition of the gasoline. The physicist indicates that there must have been an overload of energy on the engine cylinders. And the computer engineer simply closes and reopens all the windows. Everyone laughs at the joke that the IT specialist always gives the same advice: to close and reopen all windows – computer or otherwise.

Once we have their attention, we suggest a journey into the imagination to explore what the competing wall clock companies are up to. We tell them to close their eyes, choose one of their competitors, and imagine that they have the most secure lab for innovating and exploring novel solutions to address market niches. We ask them to envision the design of the laboratory, colors on the walls, the equipment, and the lab team's discussion.

After a while, we ask them to imagine that they're no longer looking at this place from outside, but that they've become one of the competitor's team members, participating in a heated discussion on what's still missing in the wall clock business. The premise for their discussion is that there's a market niche that's been overlooked – a well-hidden gem, and all that has to be done is discover it.

After 10 minutes of complete silence we ask them to return slowly to the present reality, open their eyes, and share what they've imagined. Some stories are full of tension, as the team they imagined, operating under high pressure, couldn't find any solution. Others are full of humor, with some funny ideas popping up, such as a clock that climbs up and down the wall.

One tale, however, grabbed everyone's attention: the team in this vision deliberated on why they were losing customers and came to the conclusion that the current world was interactive, while their clocks' faces are set once and stay that way forever.

Someone in this daydream commented, "OK, then why don't we offer an interactive wall clock?" Someone else added, "And why not make the clock's face a screen and use a flash memory card as to upload photos?"

This led to a flurry of discussion: perhaps the screen could be managed with a remote control, similar to TV. And why only photos? The owner should also be able to upload video to the screen/face! Someone suggested the wall clock could be linked to a portal to use the larger files stored there, like video clips, music, photos, and news. An easy-to-operate app could make it manageable from smartphones.

When the woman reporting her vision finished, everyone was silent for a moment. Then they all started talking at once, seeing incredible potential for a new line of interactive wall clocks with a manageable and adjustable screen. They immediately turned to creating an action plan to develop this idea.

Why did this powerful flow of ideas occur only after the group stepped into their competitor's shoes? Why couldn't a similar exercise related to their own business work just as well?

As we know from Chapter 19, distance helps. The less we're directly confronting the problem, the further away we are, the better chance we have to find novel solutions. Very often the novelty is not accessible through "intuitive" problem solving, or through direct A-to-B thinking. It's hidden somewhere at the fringes. Or it's stored deep in the back of our minds, a sort of dream or reminiscence of a few words heard at the bar. Pushing and confronting the problem directly doesn't reveal the undiscovered gems. To explore the peripheries, one needs imagination and an ambience that gives the mind freedom to explore.

Imagination for Personal and Family Development

Imagination opens multiple new worlds to explore.[3] You may play alone or with your family. Here are a few experiments to try:

---

[3] Neumeier (2014).

Make it a custom during the weekend to sit down with your family for imagination time. Have everyone close their eyes and imagine in silence that they are all trekking high in the mountains. Each family member imagines his or her own scenario. You may add, at some point, some additional information. Perhaps a storm is coming, or you come upon a lost tourist. Again, let everybody continue imagining in silence on their own. After a significant time interval you may suggest that you found a well-hidden cave and you all decide to explore it.

Add your own suggestions or decide to keep your interventions to a minimum. After 15 minutes or so, have everybody open their eyes and share their stories.

The next weekend you might pretend that your family has been selected for an expedition to Mars (as NASA decided not to break up families when exploring outer space), and during the imagining suggest some unexpected events. Perhaps the following weekend you might place the family among Native Americans living thousands of years ago. The tribe is preparing to move to another location, and your family is packing up your wigwam. While traveling, the tribe encounters several impediments: a deep river, high mountains, a storm. Your family gets lost but ultimately finds its way out. After opening your eyes, share how each of you imagined other family members in these situations.

It's good to remember that spatial and temporal distance helps augment creativity and stimulate brain plasticity. Add your own ideas to the scenarios. Designate heroes: your youngest daughter rescuing a kitten who fell down a well; your oldest son becoming a computer engineer.

In each session, after opening your eyes, make sure that everybody tells his or her story without interruptions. Then, after everybody has reported a story, open it up for discussion and enjoy the exchange.

Summary and Tips

Some say that imagination is the cornerstone of success. It shows things concealed at the fringes, creates empathy by letting us step into another's shoes, and becomes a pathway to envisioning possible future scenarios.[4] Imagination is a kind of "workshop for the mind," making the unthinkable real.[5] It can be a central fulcrum for creativity and divergent thinking,

---

[4] Morosini (2010); Faucette (2012).
[5] Hill (2015).

by blending diverse and usually unconnected issues, which, when merged together, may demonstrate new possibilities and a new power.

These insights are also illustrated by neuroscience. When you envision things never seen before, the mind opens up to creative thinking much more than by envisioning something familiar. This is because the brain simply has to establish new neural connections, as it can't rely on connections that have been shaped by past experience. In other words, imagining new areas provokes the brain to accommodate the unknown. And, in this case, it isn't only single neurons establishing new connections, but entire neural networks interacting with one another.[6]

Along these lines, one may conclude that imagining new, undiscovered lands augments the brain's plasticity and makes the mind open to new challenges; "the impossible becomes possible."[7] And, most importantly, it works regardless of your situation. It works whether you are in good shape or disabled, at work or at home on maternity leave, at peace or going through family upheaval, retired, traveling, or in school. Just try to project your current situation into some distant (spatially and/or temporally) scenario. This is the major difference between daydream and our imagination exercises: in the first situation you are aimlessly dreaming of alternative realities; in the latter, you explore possible scenarios in a preset framework for novel ideas and solutions.

---

[6] Kaufman (2013); Porter (2014).
[7] From Morosini (2010).

CHAPTER 25

Summary
Training Possibilitivity

It Is Trainable

You may have noticed that most of my practical suggestions for building possibilitivity, such as creating distance, using metaphors and simulations, introducing joy, dancing, practicing bodily techniques, and introducing imagination, are all related to stimulating brain plasticity and contribute to cognitive flexibility.

As we discussed before, neuroplasticity was once believed to be a trait characteristic of babies and toddlers, but we now understand that both synaptic plasticity (the appearance of new neuronal paths) and neurogenesis (where stem cells can reproduce fully functioning brain cells) occur in adults as well.

However, there has been some doubt as to whether we can *train* our brains to be more plastic. For example, can training in music influence the brain's receptivity to other types of learning? One research project documented that eight-year-old children who were given six months of musical training significantly improved their pitch processing in speech and linguistics. The focus on music, even for a relatively short period, had a powerful effect on the functional organization of the children's brains.[1] This also works for adults. Learning to play music is a highly complex task that involves the interaction of several modalities and higher-order cognitive functions. That interaction moves beyond the music to create new behavioral, structural, and functional modifications. In fact, we have considerable and consistent evidence that all sorts of mind-training activities can have a lasting impact on brain plasticity,[2] regardless of age.[3]

Like musical training, the techniques presented in this section can enhance neuroplasticity. To be effective, selected exercises must be

---

[1] Moreno et al. (2008).
[2] Herholz and Zatorre (2012); Karbach and Schubert (2013).
[3] Smith et al. (2009).

performed consistently and their practice must be maintained over time. Practiced in this way, they can have a durable effect on the propensity of the brain to react in an open, malleable way to challenges, and our possibilitivity bar will be set much higher. We could call this generalized property *meta-plasticity*, indicating that plasticity shifts to a higher-order level, with long-term effects.[4]

I recommend that you use not one, but several, of these techniques to address different modalities and to simultaneously deliver diverse neuroplasticity-stimulating impulses to the brain. I try to use them all. Joy and humor is my definite preference in whatever I do; paradoxically, the more serious the problem I face, the more humor I employ. This has an impact on two levels: it builds a positive environment for new neuronal connections, and it also helps me maintain a healthy distance from vexing impediments.

Adding metaphors opens the avenue for new insights. The Feldenkrais techniques present new sets of movements, which require new neural connections. And dancing is my favorite. Tuning into your partner's world, emotions, and kinesthetic energy engages the mind–body unity and increases brain malleability. Those are my preferences, but everyone has to find the techniques that suit them best.

Possibilitivity is then within reach, as the plastic brain and the open mind don't automatically reject challenges generally perceived as undoable. These DIY techniques are powerful, as are inspirational case studies of people doing things against all odds and succeeding by bringing system-wide solutions for profound and lasting change. Some are featured in this book, and you can easily find more examples in print and online.[5]

War Victims: A Seemingly Insurmountable Problem

Take for example the situation of millions of war victims all around the world. Marginalized and isolated, they live lives of despair. Particularly devastating are the conditions landmine victims face. Both the substance and the scope of the problem are numbing, especially given that there are more than 60 million landmines still buried in more than 80 countries. Every 22 minutes, somewhere in the world, someone steps on a landmine (often a long-forgotten one). Eighty percent of these landmine victims are civilians, half of whom are children. In 2007 alone, 5,436 people became

---

[4] Term coined by Abraham and Bear (1996).
[5] See, for example, Elkington and Hartigan (2008); Schwartz (2012); Praszkier (2018).

casualties of landmines, primarily in Africa and the Middle East. These incidents result in a pattern of victimization that creates apathy, resentment, and hatred, furthering the potential for violence across the globe.

Amputee Turns Victims into Leaders

One landmine victim was Jerry White, an American citizen who stepped on a landmine while on a weekend camping trip in the Middle East and lost his left leg. Instead of wallowing in despair, White committed himself to creating a world in which victims do not exist, because they become active survivors and leaders.[6] Convinced that no one is better equipped to break cycles of violence than those who have survived war, White launched the global Survivors Corps network, to show how survivors can rebuild their lives and communities in order to break free of the vicious cycle of victimization and violence.

Survivors Corps offers a five-step program: First, victims must "Face Facts" and accept the harsh – often permanent – reality of suffering and loss, however brutal it may be. Second, they must "Choose Life," rejecting death and letting go of resentments. "Reaching Out" is the third step, which includes finding peers, friends, and family to break the isolation and loneliness that comes in the aftermath of a crisis. Fourth, the survivors must "Get Moving," by getting into society and out of solitude. Last, they must "Give Back." As they thrive in their new reality, they must share their success and give again and again through acts of service and kindness. This perpetuates the process in which victims become leaders who help other victims become leaders and so on, creating a snowball effect around the world and in dangerous regions in particular.

By 2009, members of the Survivors Corps had made over 116,000 home and hospital visits, providing each survivor with his or her own Individual Recovery Action Plan, and in 80 percent of cases, successfully turned the victim into an active leader.

Rats Against Landmines

This program, while exceptionally powerful, is a post-incident intervention. The mines are still out there causing more casualties and creating more

---

[6] See www.ashoka.org/en/fellow/jerry-white#intro; also an interview with Jerry White at www.youtube.com/watch?time_continue=11&v=4xGAxNSBCkA (both retrieved March 16, 2019).

victims. The problem is that demining is difficult. It must be performed by teams of experts. It's very expensive, and it puts human life at risk.

Bart Weetjens addressed this problem head-on. Seeing the vast number of contaminated with hidden landmines and other explosive remnants of war, and that the resulting tragic accidents hamper communities from developing their productive land, he decided to find an easy, cheap, and fast way to demine, that would be scalable for areas of particular need, such as Africa.[7]

Weetjens's solution? Rats. He simply trained rats to detect explosives in minutes amounts. A rat scans on average 100 square meters in half an hour, twice the area covered by a demining expert in a day. So far, tests have shown that two rats can analyze 320 samples in 40 minutes. It would take an entire day for eight highly skilled technicians to analyze the same quantity. Also, in comparison to mine detection using dogs, rats are much cheaper and weigh much less, so they are not as endangered as heavier and slower dogs.

Moving from an old, rented laboratory in Belgium, Bart Weetjens relocated his lab to Tanzania in East Africa, where he set up a world-class training facility in Morogoro, 190 kilometers from Dar es Salaam. He used the local rats, which were easy to collect for virtually no cost, and, instead of waiting for expensive human experts, he trained local citizens to assist. This provided jobs for an economically disadvantaged group while keeping costs low.

Bart Weetjens's demining efforts were successful, and his locally driven solution proved efficient and scalable, and contributed to local development. He was elected as one of the global Architects of Peace[8] and now works closely with the Geneva International Center for Humanitarian Demining to spread his approach globally.

Summary and Tips

Jerry White and Bart Weetjens addressed one of the most critical issues of human health and safety. For others, this may have seemed undoable, but that didn't stop these two from taking a leap of faith and developing novel solutions. Their minds were open, and they were ready to tackle intractable challenges.

---

[7] See www.ashoka.org/en/fellow/bart-weetjens#intro (retrieved March 16, 2019).
[8] See www.architectsofpeace.org/architects-of-peace/bart-weetjens (retrieved March 16, 2019).

In this part we presented a full palette of techniques to foster the mind's openness. These techniques are accessible to everyone, including the disabled. Remember: simply imagining that you are dancing or observing others dance can create new neural pathways. And humor and joy are available to everyone. I've rarely met anyone with as fine a sense of humor or more positive attitude than my wheelchair-bound friend, Piotr Pawłowski.

Remember, to augment your own neuroplasticity and propensity for perceiving challenges as doable, you don't need arduous training and forceful effort. The more subtle the stimulations, the more the brain is prone to respond with new neural connections.

The prerequisite is an environment full of joy and humor, no matter what conditions you face. Play with metaphors. Have fun with games and simulations. And let your imagination take flight.

Précis

What we can or cannot do, what we consider possible or impossible, is rarely a function of our true capability. It is more likely a function of our beliefs about who we are. (Anthony Robbins)[1]

It's kind of fun to do the impossible. (Walt Disney)

Remember Bruce Springsteen singing:

> I straighten the back and I'm working on a dream
> I'm working on a dream
> Come on!
> I'm working on a dream
> Though sometimes it feels so far away
> I'm working on a dream
> And I know it will be mine someday.[2]

The Lady Who Did Not Behave Properly

Oh Lord, may I be directed what to do and what to leave undone. (Elizabeth Fry)

I continue to be fascinated by people who "straighten their back and are working on their dreams." Imagine, for example, a young woman from a family of Quaker bankers during the Georgian/Victorian era. You might expect that she would behave according to the many rules and expectations shaping women's lives at that time. But Elizabeth Fry (born 1780) didn't comply with these rigorous norms. Driven by her sensitivity to poverty and injustice, she visited a women's prison, where she was horrified by the overcrowded living conditions of the women and children, some of whom had been held for years without trial. She returned the next day with food

---

[1] Author of *Unlimited Power: The New Science of Personal Achievement* (Robbins, 1997).
[2] See www.youtube.com/watch?v=R3ZMfPXgd_M (retrieved March 16, 2019).

and clothes and continued to visit, often staying overnight, in order to experience and understand first-hand the conditions there.

Fry's dream was to eradicate social injustice and extreme poverty, and, believing it was achievable, she pursued it against all odds. Her first impulse was to improve the prisoners' conditions by bringing in basic supplies. But she also talked with the women to convince them to care for themselves, self-organize, and vote for their representatives.

In the long run, her willingness to raise an unpopular topic others would have preferred to avoid led her to establish the first nationwide women's organization in Britain dedicated to caring for female prisoners.[3] Fry also became the first woman to give evidence at a House of Commons committee, during an inquiry into conditions in British prisons. In 1825, she published an influential book,[4] which gave an account based on her observations and on the legal status of female prisoners at the time. This laid the groundwork for penal reforms.

Fry was a role model for many future women activists, including Octavia Hill (born 1838), who was particularly concerned with the welfare of the inhabitants of overpopulated cities and initiated the development of housing for the poor.

Changing the Inner-City from Within

> Trust your passion, identify your dreams, and find the courage to share them with others, no matter how many times they call you a fool. (Bill Strickland)

Bill Strickland (born 1947) grew up in a low-income, inner-city neighborhood in Pittsburgh. As a self-described "black kid growing up in a bad neighborhood," he understood all about the hopelessness of the ghetto. His dream from a young age was to help other kids thrive and develop their talents and potential. He also followed his own passion to study, and in 1969, graduated *cum laude* from the University of Pittsburgh with a degree in American history and foreign relations.

During his schooling, Strickland was continuously involved in his neighborhood community of Manchester. In 1968, while still in college, he founded the Manchester Craftsmen's Guild to bring arts education and mentorship to the inner-city youth. This evolved (in 1972) into the

---

[3] Association for the Reformation of the Female Prisoners in Newgate, later renamed to: British Ladies' Society for Promoting the Reformation of Female Prisoners.

[4] *Observations on the Visiting, Superintendence, and Government, of Female Prisoners* (Fry, 2018).

Bidwell Training Center,[5] a nationally accredited career training institution offering programs in fields ranging from horticulture to medical sciences.

For decades, Strickland has been passionately involved in developing programs for kids and adults in inner cities. His courses in ceramics, photography, and painting draw in hundreds of kids a year, 90 percent of whom receive high school diplomas and enroll in college. Adults also receive career training in the culinary arts, pharmacology, horticultural technology, and other fields, through partnerships with major corporations in the area. The Bidwell Training Center includes a 350-seat jazz auditorium, a 40,000-square-foot greenhouse covering half a city block, a state-of-the-art chemistry lab, a full-scale ceramics department, and a culinary institute.

As a result of his work, Strickland has received a MacArthur Fellowship "Genius Grant." He has also lectured at the Harvard Graduate School of Education and served on the board of the National Endowment for the Arts.

The title of his most popular publication is absolutely fitting from our book's perspective: *Make the Impossible Possible: One Man's Crusade to Inspire Others to Dream Bigger and Achieve the Extraordinary.*[6] In it, Strickland tells the story of how he spent more than 30 years transforming the lives of thousands of people, thus making the impossible possible.

The Girl Who Stood Up Against Her Tribe

Imagine a nomadic, tribal, and male-dominated community situated miles away from any town. There's a girl there who sees the value of education and wishes to pursue her own schooling beyond the minimum level. To do so, she has to stand up in front of a gathering of elderly men, who respond to her request with a firm "no." Even her own mother is completely opposed to the idea, arguing that education runs counter to a woman's traditional role and could bring a curse on the family.

But all of this didn't stop Ndinini Kimesera Sikar of the Maasai tribe from enrolling in school. The tribe objected, and sometimes she needed a police escort to get to class. But she persisted, telling her family and other tribal members how she saw the world and how it might be changed.

Despite the objections of her tribe, Sikar went on to graduate from university and landed a high-paying job at a bank in Dar es Salaam. She frequently returned to her community and eventually convinced the tribe she

---

[5] See http://manchesterbidwell.org/ (retrieved March 16, 2019).
[6] Strickland and Rause (2009).

was on the right track, not because of the money she earned, but because of the few goats she brought back with her. For a community with an economy based on breeding livestock, goats are a symbol of success. The tribe finally understood that education could lead to property ownership and personal empowerment for women. It was the first step in a cultural shift that gave girls the opportunity to go to school.

At this point Sikar decided to leave her well-paid job at the bank and move to Arusia, a town located in the middle of the Maasai population. In 2000, she initiated (together with two other women) the Maasai Women Development Organization (MWEDO),[7] to support women's access to education, health, and economic and cultural rights. For the very first time, Maasai women in Tanzania had decided to establish an organization they could call their own. Their group empowers women to support sustainable, equitable, and humane development, through access to education, economic empowerment, and maternal health and HIV/AIDS education. Today, MWEDO has more than 5,000 women members from the Arusha and Manyara regions of Tanzania.

I interviewed Sikar in May 2005, and ever since then I've kept in the back of my mind the image of that little girl standing lonely in front of the gathering of the Maasai elders, trying to convince them to let her go to school. I'll always admire how strong her conviction must have been to empower her to pursue her vision against all odds, especially against tradition and her own family, and how smart and committed she was to return and show them the value of education for girls.

"He Who Sows Utopia Will Reap Reality"

Slow Food unites the pleasure of food with responsibility, sustainability and harmony with nature. (Carlo Petrini)

Food history is as important as a baroque church. Governments should recognize cultural heritage and protect traditional foods. A cheese is as worthy of preserving as a sixteenth-century building. (Carlo Petrini)

I believe that he who sows utopia will reap reality. (Carlo Petrini)

Eating as a cultural phenomenon is deeply embedded in Carlo Petrini's history. As the Italian chef and activist said in one of his interviews, he "grew up in a place where social events and leisure time are mostly related

---

[7] See http://maasaiwomentanzania.com/ (retrieved March 16, 2019).

to food. Food was and still is an essential aspect of the festivities and conviviality of Piedmont traditions, like singing and dancing, and thus growing up I became aware of this cultural, social and historical aspect of food, which was starting to be threatened by a false idea of modernity."[8]

Petrini simply couldn't agree with the fast-food and fast-life philosophy beginning to prevail globally. He imagined a utopian world in which all people can access and enjoy food that is good for them, good for those who grow it, and good for the planet. He started "sowing this utopia" in the early 1980s, beginning with Arcigola, an association whose aim was to promote the culture of conviviality of good food and wine.

A critical life-shaping moment happened for him in 1986, when he and his friends opposed the opening of the first McDonald's restaurant on the Piazza di Spagna in the heart of Rome. Demonstrating against fast-food at the famous Spanish Steps, he realized that opposing and defying was not his way. He decided that instead of confronting multi-national corporations head-on, he would create resistance by building awareness of the goodness of the traditional food that was at risk. And this is how his ideas and the Arcigola experience developed into the Slow Food movement. In 1989, at the Opéra Comique in Paris, the Slow Food Manifesto was signed by more than 20 delegations from around the world, and Petrini was elected president, an office that he still holds today. The Manifesto mentions:

- Good quality, flavorsome, and healthy food.
- Clean production that does not harm the environment.
- Fair, accessible prices for consumers, and fair conditions and pay for producers.

Ultimately, Arcigola advocates for good, clean, and fair quality as an act of civilization and a pledge for a better future.

Petrini's motto quoted above says that "he who sows utopia will reap reality." And indeed, the Slow Food idea spread throughout the world, engaging millions of people in 2,000 food communities in more than 160 countries. Slow Food is not only about the culture of eating, but also about the small-scale and sustainable production of quality food and the way it's distributed and sold. The idea has spread through the global indigenous Terra Madre Food Communities Network, which connects with a diverse range of networks, communities and organizations around the world, and

---

[8] See www.yesmagazine.org/issues/how-to-eat-like-our-lives-depend-on-it/an-interview-with-carlo-petrini (retrieved March 16, 2019).

has even reached out to youth through the Slow Food Youth Network (SFYN).

Slow Food evolves in various countries according to the cultural context and local initiatives. For example, in the United States there is an open Slow Food resource center called Ark of Taste, where people can nominate rigorous criteria slow food must meet.[9]

I had the privilege and pleasure to talk to Carlo Pertini in August 2008,[10] and was amazed by his passion and visionary thinking. He had just coined the term eco-gastronomy and was very engaged in developing his University of Gastronomic Sciences (UNISG, launched in 2004), a school bridging the gap between agriculture and eco-gastronomy.

Petrini was *Time Magazine*'s Hero of the Year in 2004, was named one of the "50 people who could save the planet" by the British newspaper the *Guardian* in 2008, received the highest UN Environmental Award of the Champion of the Earth (2013), and was named "Special Ambassador Zero Hunger for Europe" by the Food and Agriculture Organization of the United Nations (2016). He was also nominated as Communicator of the Year at the International Wine and Spirit Competition in London, received the Sicco Mansholt Prize in the Netherlands, an honorary degree in cultural anthropology from the University of New Hampshire, and the Eckart Witzigmann Science and Media Prize from the Witzigmann Academy in Germany.

Pertini's Slow Food movement has influenced culture beyond the world of food and gastronomy. It inspired the Slow Web movement, which opposes the habit of high-speed web browsing and the crush of digital information overload and encourages us to be more deliberate in our intake of information.[11] The Slow Web approach, recognized by Wiki as an overall shift in human culture, aims to make connectivity manageable in real-time.[12]

Making the Impossible Happen

Elizabeth Fry, Bill Strickland, Ndinini Sikar, and Carlo Petrini pursued their dreams far beyond what was commonly perceived as realizable. So did

[9] See www.slowfoodusa.org/ark-of-taste-in-the-usa (retrieved March 16, 2019).
[10] I interviewed him as a Senior Fellow candidate to Ashoka; see www.ashoka.org/en/fellow/carlo-petrini#intro (retrieved March 16, 2019).
[11] See https://en.wikipedia.org/wiki/Slow_movement_(culture) (retrieved March 16, 2019).
[12] See Jack Cheng's, the Slow Web's initiator's, article at https://jackcheng.com/the-slow-web/ (retrieved March 16, 2019).

the many other individuals featured in this book: those who turned disabilities into a powerful fulcrum for doing good (Piotr Pawłowski, Temple Grandin, Preeda Limmontakul, Jerry White), shaped their businesses to be full of joy and bottom-up initiatives (Ricardo Semler, Chris Rufer, Dennis W. Bakke), and introduced large-scale, system-changing innovations (Mary Gordon, Lucy Chagnon, Bart Weetjens, Bill Strickland).

My message here is that you can meet similar challenges. But while this book is about augmenting the mind's propensity to perceive difficult challenges as doable, it would of course be naïve to think that everything is possible and that the only constraints are in our minds. Obviously there are things that are objectively undoable, at least at this time – for example: eradicating corporate greed, eliminating polluting industries, bringing fair education to all kids globally, or changing an authoritarian boss's character. We need to differentiate between things impartially or temporarily undoable and those extremely difficult challenges that are in fact doable. And this can be done effectively only when the mind is not biased in one direction, either toward the doable or the undoable. Neither extreme is desirable; people who are careless risk-takers are simply dangerous (for themselves and their environment), while those who are overly rational and skeptical not only suppress their own and others' innovations, but are simply boring.

To deepen our understanding of what may counteract and what may foster the conviction of doability, we demonstrated the most likely psychological and sociological mechanisms involved. A lack of brain malleability, the need to keep cognition consistent, majority influence, a reliance solely on strong ties, and a lack of creativity and "sync" all inhibit possibilitivity. Conversely, brain plasticity throughout life, complexity thinking, minority influence, weak ties with an array of acquaintances, horizontal networks, and nurtured creativity and sync all support our ability to see things as doable.

This theoretical deliberation led us to a portfolio of possibilitivity-enhancing and training methods, including the role of distance and metaphors, games and simulations, joy and dance, bodily techniques, and imagination.

It's a lot to chew on, but this book is only a first step toward understanding the mechanisms that lead us to perceive a challenge as doable or not doable. New research in related fields is accelerating. For example, in 2018, neuroscientists discovered that highly creative people use connections among brain regions that usually work in opposition to each other, thus creating functional large-scale brain networks.[13] This may

---

[13] Beaty et al. (2018).

lead to further exploration of ways to stimulate the simultaneous arousal of basic brain networks.

One last caveat: I don't want to leave the impression that I think it's better to be continuously activated, and never stop innovating and facing challenges. In many situations, I would rather opt for Carlo Pertini's Slow Life philosophy. Like yin and yang, it's good to have periods of quality withdrawal, whether in the wilderness or in a hammock, to contrast with periods of activation. To gain the full benefit of both states, choose them deliberately and purposefully. It's better not to retreat to the wilderness to hide from the challenges of life, or to remain hyperactive because you don't know any other way to be. Make conscious choices suitable for the moment, and know that with practiced possibilitivity, you can achieve whatever it is that you desire.

Appendix: Measuring Possibilitivity

Introduction

It occurred to me that academicians might be interested in measuring the propensity for perceiving challenges as doable. The following appendix introduces a methodology for constructing a measurement tool to help assess the level of possibilitivity.

I've decided to make these methodological concepts available prior to completing the study and publishing the results. I simply disagree with the academic sector's typical practice of discussing concepts and methods only after an article has been published, thereby delaying practical use of the information for six years or more (consider: a year for raising funds, another two to three years for carrying out the research, and a year or two waiting for the article to be published). I envision an academic world in which the social sciences nurture an early exchange of ideas and inspirations, and in doing so, become much more nimble and agile, especially given that in the physical sciences and mathematics early-sharing platforms already exist.[1] It's worth considering to what degree could this openness speed the development of human science.

Abstract

Assuming that people have an attribute which I have called their "possibilitivity level" (P-level), i.e., the extent to which they view difficult tasks as doable, we are called upon to measure this trait. To do so, we will construct a questionnaire that asks subjects to relate to a few stories about difficult situations in the areas of business, social, and personal life. The stories should depict challenging situations that are neither so difficult that subjects will quickly see them as unsolvable, nor so easy that subjects will

---

[1] E.g., ArXive, Mathoverflow, Polymath.

rate them as obviously doable. In that vein, the challenge is to identify three stories rated as having "medium difficulty."

The P-questionnaire will include the three identified stories followed by several Likert-type-scale questions related to the subject's opinion on the level of doability. The assumption is that the subjects will identify with the heroes of the presented stories and reflect on their actions while scoring their own reaction to similar situations.

The questionnaire will be validated across diverse groups.

First Step: Identifying Stories

Businesspeople and social activists will be asked to sketch a short delineation of a situation from their professional experience which they found difficult or challenging. Some individuals will also be asked for similar stories on difficult situations from their personal life. The plan is to address between six and eight persons from each of the three categories, yielding a total of 24–32 stories.

Next, a few (between three and six) neutral raters will be asked to rate all the stories on two Likert-type scales: difficult – easy and solvable – unsolvable. Three stories – each about a business, social, and personal situation of medium difficulty – will be selected. These selected stories will be shaped from the perspective of "a hero," i.e., someone (John, Mary, Steve, etc.) who is facing the problem and trying to find a way to solve it.

Second Step: Constructing the Questionnaire

For each story, a Likert-style list of statements related to the P-level will be constructed. Examples of questions include, "I think that John will finally succeed," or "I think that this situation is solvable," shaped in direct or reverse way, e.g., "I see no chance for Mary to accomplish what she wanted." Some neutral questions will be added and, finally, all questions will be randomized. The total number of questions per story should not exceed 12.

Third Step: Validation

Validation will occur across diverse target groups, e.g., graduate students, business startup founders, social activists, etc. Finally, it will be tested within a population's random sample $N^\circ \approx 1000$, which will reveal the societal standard tendencies.

Fourth Step: Using the P-level Questionnaire for Research

The first line of studies will assume that P-level is an independent variable consistent over time and situations for each person. It will focus on finding possible dependent variables that show differences between individuals with high and low P-level, e.g., life satisfaction, creativity, propensity for building social capital. Additionally, individuals from different professions or with different means of engagement may be compared for their average level of possibilitivity.

The second line will assume the P-level as a dependent variable and study what factors may contribute to its augmentation within an individual, e.g., measuring the P-level results after creativity training or techniques aimed at augmenting brain plasticity, or after intensive internships with dynamic social programs.

References

Abel, M. H. (2002). Humor, stress, and coping strategies. *Humor – International Journal of Humor Research*, 15(4): 365–381.

Abraham, W. C. & Bear, M. F. (1996). Metaplasticity: The plasticity of synaptic plasticity. *Trends in Neurosciences*, 19(4): 126–130.

Adler, P. S. & Kwon, S.-W. (2002). Social capital: Prospects for a new concept. *Academy of Management Review*, 27(1): 17–40.

Albert, S., Ashforth, B. E., & Dutton, J. E. (2000). Organizational identity and identification: Charting new waters and building new bridges. *Academy of Management Review*, 25(1): 13–17.

Alexander, F. M. (1984). *The Use of the Self*. London: Orion.

Alfaro, A., Bernabeu, A., Agulló, C., Parra, J., & Fernández, E. (2015). Hearing colors: An example of brain plasticity. *Frontiers in System Neuroscience*, 9(56): 1–9.

Amabile, T. M., Barsade, S. G., Mueller, J. S., & Staw, B. M. (2005). Affect and creativity at work. *Administrative Science Quarterly*, 50(3): 367–403.

Andel, P. Van (1994). Anatomy of the unsought finding. Serendipity: Origin, history, domains, traditions, appearances, patterns and programmability. *British Journal for the Philosophy of Science*, 45(2): 631–648.

Asch, S. E. (1956). Studies of independence and conformity: I. A minority of one against a unanimous majority. *Psychological Monographs: General and Applied*, 70(9): 1–70.

Ash, T. G. (2002). *The Polish Solidarity*. New Haven, CT: Yale University Press.

Axelrod, R. & Cohen, M. D. (2000). *Harnessing Complexity: Organizational Implications of a Social Frontier*. New York: Basic Books.

Baer, D. (2017). People naturally sync their bodies, breathing – and skin. *Science of Us*. Retrieved July 10, 2018 from: http://nymag.com/scienceofus/2017/01/how-interpersonal-synchrony-works.html

Baker, H. & Fultz, A. (2010). Motivating students in inner city schools. Miami University. Retrieved June 29, 2017 from: http://performancepyramid.miamioh.edu/node/1188

Bakke, D. W. (2006). *Joy at Work: A Revolutionary Approach to Fun on the Job*. Seattle, WA: Pear Press.

Barabási, A. L. (2003). *Linked: How Everything Is Connected to Everything Else and What It Means for Business, Science, and Everyday Life.* Cambridge, MA: A Plume Book.

Barnes, J. H. (1984). Cognitive biases and their impact on strategic planning. *Strategic Management,* 5(2): 129–137.

Barron, F. (1968). *Creativity and Personal Freedom.* New York: Van Nostrand Reinhold.

Barsade, S. G. (2002). The ripple effect: Emotional contagion and its influence on group behavior. *Administrative Science Quarterly,* 47(4): 644–675.

Beaty, R. E., Kenett, Y. N., Christensen, A. P., Rosenberg, M. D., Benedek, M., Chen, Q., Fink, A., Qiu, J., Kwapil, T. R., Kane, M. J., & Silvia, P. J. (2018). Robust prediction of individual creative ability from brain functional connectivity. *Proceedings of the National Academy of Sciences of the United States of America,* 115(5): 1087–1092.

Bem, D. J. (1967). Self-perception: An alternative interpretation of cognitive dissonance phenomena. *Psychological Review,* 74(3): 183–200.

Benedek, M., Beaty, R., Jauk, E., Koschutnig, K., Fink, A., Silvia, P. J., Dunst, B., & Neubauer, A. C. (2014). Creating metaphors: The neural basis of figurative language production. *NeuroImage,* 90(100): 99–106.

Berger, P. L. & Luckmann, T. (1967). *The Social Construction of Reality.* Garden City, NY: Anchor.

Bergland C. (2013). Why is dancing so good for your brain? *Psychology Today.* Retrieved April 13, 2018 from: www.psychologytoday.com/us/blog/the-athletes-way/201310/why-is-dancing-so-good-your-brain

Beversdorf, D. Q. (2013). Pharmacological effects on creativity. In: Vartanian, O. & Bristol. A. S. (Eds.), *Neuroscience of Creativity* (pp. 151–173). Cambridge, MA: The MIT Press.

Bock, L. (2015). *Work Rules! Insights from Inside Google That Will Transform How You Live and Lead.* New York: Twelve.

Bornstein, D. (2004). *How to Change the World: Social Entrepreneurs and the Power of New Ideas.* New York: Oxford University Press.

Bovee, C. L. & Thill, J. V. (2011). *Business Communication Today.* Boston, MA: Pearson.

Bowen, M. (1978). *Family Therapy in Clinical Practice.* New York: Aronson.

Brewer, M. B. & Gardner, W. L. (1996). Who is this "we"? Levels of collective identity and self representations. *Journal of Personality and Social Psychology,* 71(1): 83–93.

Brown, B. (2003). *The Private Revolution: Women in the Polish Underground Movement.* London: Hera Trust.

Burt, R. S. (1997). The contingent value of social capital. *Administrative Science Quarterly,* 42(2): 339–365.

Buza, H., Jedliński, K., Praszkier, R., Rogowska, A., Samson, A., & Wroniszewski, M. (1976). *Psychosocial Treatment and Rehabilitation of Young Adult Schizophrenic Patients.* Warsaw: Family Therapy Center Synapsis.

Cameron, K. & Lavine, M. (2006). *Making the Impossible Possible: Leading Extraordinary Performance – The Rocky Flats Story*. San Francisco, CA: Berrett-Koehler.

Caudron, S. (1992). Humor is healthy in the workplace. *Personnel Journal*, 71(6): 63–66.

Chermahini, S. A. & Hommel, B. (2010). The (b)link between creativity and dopamine: Spontaneous eye blink rates predict and dissociate divergent and convergent thinking. *Cognition*, 115(3): 458–465.

Christensen, J. F., Gomila, A., Gaigg, S. B., Sivarajah, N., & Calvo-Merino, B. (2016). Dance expertise modulates behavioral and psychophysiological responses to affective body movement. *Journal of Experimental Psychology: Human Perception and Performance*, 42(8): 1139–1147.

Cialdini, R. B. & Goldstein, N. J. (2004). Social influence: Compliance and conformity. *Annual Review of Psychology*, 55: 591–621.

Coleman, J. S. (1988). Social capital in the creation of human capital. *American Journal of Sociology*, 94: 95–12.

Csermely, P. (2009). *Weak Links: The Universal Key to the Stability of Networks and Complex Systems*. Berlin: Springer Verlag.

Csíkszentmihályi, M. (1991). *Flow: The Psychology of Optimal Experience*. New York: Harper Perennial.

Csíkszentmihályi, M. (1997a). *Creativity: Flow and the Psychology of Discovery and Intention*. New York: Harper Perennial.

Csíkszentmihályi, M. (1997b). Happiness and creativity. *Futurist*, 31(5): 8–12.

Daft, R. L. (2015). *Organization Theory and Design*. Boston, MA: Cengage Learning.

Darbellay, F., Moody, Z., Sedooka, A., & Steffen, G. (2014). Interdisciplinary research boosted by serendipity. *Creativity Research Journal*, 26(1): 1–10.

Darling, N. (2010). Facebook and the strength of weak ties. *Psychology Today*. Retrieved July 10, 2018 from: www.psychologytoday.com/blog/thinking-about-kids/201005/facebook-and-the-strength-weak-ties

Davis, G. A. (1993). Personalities of creative people. *R&D Innovator*, 2(4). Retrieved July 9, 2018 from: www.winstonbrill.com/bril001/html/article_index/articles/1–50/article34_body.html

De Drue, C. K. W. & De Vries, N. K. (2001). Group consensus and minority influence. In De Drue, C. K. W. & De Vries, N. K. (Eds.), *Group Consensus and Minority Influence: Implications for Innovation* (pp. 1–14). Oxford: Blackwell.

Denhardt, R. B. & Denhardt, J. V. (2015). *The Dance of Leadership: The Art of Leading in Business, Government, and Society*. London: Routledge.

Dennison, P. E. (1989). *Brain Gym: Teacher's Edition*. Ventura, CA: Edu-Kinesthetics.

Doidge, N. (2007). *The Brain That Changes Itself: Stories of Personal Triumph from the Frontiers of Brain Science*. New York. Penguin Books.

Dorsey, D. (2000). Positive deviant. *Fast Company*. Retrieved December 16, 2017, from: www.fastcompany.com/42075/positive-deviant

Draganski, B., Gaser, C., Kempermann, G., Kuhn, H. G., Winkler. J., Büchel, C., & May, A. (2006). Temporal and spatial dynamics of brain structure changes during extensive learning. *Journal of Neuroscience*, 26(23): 6314–6317.

Duhigg, C. (2016). What Google learned from its quest to build the perfect team. *New York Times Magazine*. Retrieved July 10, 2018 from: www.nytimes.com/2016/02/28/magazine/what-google-learned-from-its-quest-to-build-the-perfect-team.html

Dweck, C. S. (2006). *Mindset: The New Psychology of Success*. New York: Random House.

Eareckson-Tady, Joni (1980). *A Step Further*. Grand Rapid, MI: Zondervan.

Elkington, J. & Hartigan, P. (2008). *The Power of Unreasonable People*. Boston, MA: Harvard Business Press.

Erikson, E. H. (1993). *Childhood and Society*. New York: W. W. Norton & Company.

Evans, B. (2013). How autism became autism. *History of the Human Sciences*, 26(3): 3–31.

   (2014). The foundations of autism. *Bulletin of the History of Medicine*, 88(2): 253–285.

Faria, A. J. (1998). Business simulation games: Current usage levels – an update. *Simulation and Gaming*, 29(3): 295–308.

Faucette, J. (2012). The power of business imagination. *Entrepreneur, Europe*. Retrieved May 31, 2018 from: www.entrepreneur.com/article/223429

Feldenkrais, M. (2002). *The Potent Self: A Study of Spontaneity and Compulsion*. Berkeley, CA: Frog Books.

   (2005). *Body and Mature Behavior*. Berkeley, CA: Frog Books.

Festinger, L. (1957). *A Theory of Cognitive Dissonance*. Stanford, CA: Stanford University Press.

Festinger, L., Riecken, H. W., & Schachter, S. (2009). *When Prophecy Fails*. London: Pinter & Martin.

Fisher, L. M. (2005). Ricardo Semler won't take control. *Business Thought Leaders*. Retrieved January 31, 2017 from: www.strategy-business.com/article/05408?gko=3291c

Flaherty, A. W. (2005). Frontotemporal and dopaminergic control of idea generation and creative drive. *Journal of Comparative Neurology*, 493(1): 147–153.

Förster, J., Epstude, K., & Özelse, A. (2009). Why love has wings and sex has not: How reminders of love and sex influence creative and analytic thinking. *Personality and Social Psychology Bulletin*, 35(11): 1479–1491.

Fotuhi, O., Fong, G. T., Zanna, M. P., Borland, R., Yong, H.-H., & Cummings, K. M. (2013). Patterns of cognitive dissonance-reducing beliefs among smokers: A longitudinal analysis from the International Tobacco Control (ITC) Four Country Survey. *Tobacco Control*, 22(1): 52–58.

Fraleigh, S. H. (1998). *Dance and the Lived Body: A Descriptive Aesthetics*. Pittsburg: University of Pittsburg Press.

Fritz, G. & Werther, A. (2013). When black swans aren't: On better recognition, assessment, and forecasting of large scale, large impact, and rare event change. *Risk Management and Insurance Review*, 16(1): 1–23.

Fry, E. (2018). *Observations on the Visiting, Superintendence, and Government, of Female Prisoners*. Bel Air, CA: Forgotten Books.

Fuda, P. (2016). *Leadership Transformed: How Ordinary Managers Become Extraordinary Leaders*. Las Vegas, NV: Amazon Publishing.

Fuller, S. (2018). Advantages & disadvantages for using role play as a training method. *Bizfluent*. Retrieved February 24, 2018 from: https://bizfluent.com/info-12027484-advantages-disadvantages-using-role-play-training-method.html

Gallagher, S. (2009). Two problems of intersubjectivity. *Journal of Consciousness Studies*, 16(6–8): 289–308.

Gaser, C. & Schlaug, G. (2003). Brain structures differ between musicians and non-musicians. *Journal of Neuroscience*, 23(27): 9240–9245.

Gerrow, K. & Triller, A. (2010). Synaptic stability and plasticity in a floating world. *Current Opinion in Neurobiology*, 20(5): 631–639.

Google EMEA Engineering Hub (2009). *ArchDaily*. Retrieved July 10, 2018 from: www.archdaily.com/41400/google-emea-engineering-hub-camezind-evolution

Gordon, M. (2005). *Roots of Empathy: Changing the World Child by Child*. Toronto: Thomas Allen.

Grandin, T. (2006a). *Animals in Translation*. New York: Harcourt.

(2006b). *Thinking in Pictures: My Life with Autism*. New York: Vintage.

Granovetter, M. S. (1973). The strength of weak ties. *American Journal of Sociology*, 78(6): 1360–1380.

(1983). The strength of weak ties: A network theory revisited. *Sociological Theory*, 1(1): 201–233.

(1995). *Getting a Job: A Study of Contacts and Careers*. Chicago, IL: University of Chicago Press.

Grant, S. (2013). Top 10 instances of mob mentality. *Listverse*. Retrieved July 9, 2018 from: http://listverse.com/2013/07/28/top-10-instances-of-mob-mentality/

Green, C. S. & Bavelier, D. (2008). Exercising your brain: A review of human brain plasticity and training-induced learning. *Psychology and Aging*, 23(4): 692–701.

Gregory, A. F., Isen, A. M., & Turken, A. U. (1999). A neuropsychological theory of positive affect and its influence on cognition. *Psychological Review*, 106(3): 529–550.

Gu, Y., Janoschka, S., & Ge. S. (2013). Neurogenesis and hippocampal plasticity in adult brain. *Current Topics in Behavioral Neurosciences*, 15: 31–48.

Guilford, J. P. (1950). Creativity. *American Psychologist*, 5(9): 444–454.

Hamel, G. (2007). *The Future of Management*. Boston, MA: Harvard Business Review Press.

Hanson, K. (1988). Prospects for the good life: Education and perceptive imagination. In: Egan, K. & Nadaner, D. (Eds.), *Imagination and Education* (pp. 128–140). New York: Teachers College Press.

Hardin, C. D. & Higgins, E. T. (1996). Shared reality: How social verification makes the subjective objective. In: Sorrentino, R. M. & Higgins, E. T.

(Eds.), *Handbook of Motivation and Cognition: The Interpersonal Context*, vol. 3 (pp. 28–84). New York: Guilford Press.

Hasson, U., Ghazanfar, A. A., Galantucci, B., Garrod, S., & Keysers C. (2012). Brain-to-brain coupling: A mechanism for creating and sharing a social world. *Trends in Cognitive Science*, 16(2): 114–121.

Haun, D. B. M., van Leeuwen, E. J. C., & Edelson, M. G. (2013). Majority influence in children and other animals. *Developmental Cognitive Neuroscience*, 3: 61–71.

Hawkes, C. H. (1992). Endorphins: The basis of pleasure? *Journal of Neurology, Neurosurgery and Psychiatry*, 55(4): 247–250.

Henman, L. D. (2001). Humor as a coping mechanism: Lessons from POWs. *Humor: International Journal of Humor Research*, 14(1): 83–94.

Herholz, S. C. & Zatorre, R. J. (2012). Musical training as a framework for brain plasticity: Behavior, function, and structure. *Neuron*, 76(3): 486–502.

Herman, P. (2010). *The HIP Investor*. Hoboken, NJ: Wiley.

Hill, L. A., Brandeau, G., Truelove, E., & Lineback, K. (2014). The inescapable paradox of managing creativity. *Harvard Business Review*. Retrieved July 10, 2018 from: https://hbr.org/2014/12/the-inescapable-paradox-of-managing-creativity

Hill, N. (2015). *Think and Grow Rich*. Anderson, SC: The Mindpower Press.

Ingersoll, R. M. (2001). Teacher turnover and teacher shortages: An organizational analysis. *American Educational Research Journal*, 38(3): 499–534.

Inkson, K. (2002). Thinking creatively about careers: The use of metaphor. In: Peiperl, M., Arthur, M., Goffee, R., & Anand, N. (Eds.), *Career Creativity* (pp. 15–34). New York: Oxford University Press.

Isen, A. M., Daubman, K. A., & Nowicki, G. P. (1987). Positive affect facilitates creative problem solving. *Journal of Personality and Social Psychology*, 52: 1122–1131.

Iversen, K. (2013). *Full Body Burden: Growing Up in the Nuclear Shadow of Rocky Flats*. New York: Random House.

Jain, S., Janssen, K., & DeCelle, S. (2004). Alexander technique and Feldenkrais method: A critical overview. *Physical Medicine and Rehabilitation Clinics of North America*, 15(4): 811–825.

James, L. E. (2004). Meeting Mr. Farmer versus meeting a farmer: Specific effects of aging on learning proper names. *Psychology and Aging*, 19(3): 515–522.

Jäncke, L. (2009). The plastic human brain. *Restorative Neurology and Neuroscience*, 27(5): 521–538.

Jankowski, K., Andrzejewska, E., Endicott, J., Frączek, A., Jankowska, K., Kozłowski, S., Markiewicz, L., & Reykowski, J. (1975). *Effects of Psycho-, Kinesi-, and Pharmacotherapy in Emotional Disturbed Adolescents as Evaluated with Psychological and Physiological Methods*. Garwolin: Child Neuropsychiatric Hospital.

Jaspars, J. & Fincham, F. D. (1983). *Attribution Theory and Research: Conceptual Developmental and Social Dimensions*. Harahan, LA: Academic Press.

Jia, L., Hirt, E. R., & Karpen, S. C. (2009). Lessons from a faraway land: The effect of spatial distance on creative cognition. *Journal of Experimental Social Psychology*, 45(5): 1127–1131.

Johansson, B. B. (2004). Brain plasticity in health and disease. *Keio Journal of Medicine*, 53(4): 231–246.

Joseph, C. (2018). Advantages & disadvantages of a vertical & horizontal organization. *Chron*. Retrieved July 9, 2018 from: http://smallbusiness.chron.com/advantages-disadvantages-vertical-horizontal-organization-24212.html

Julie, A., Markham, J. A., & Greenough, W. T. (2004). Experience-driven brain plasticity: Beyond the synapse. *Neuron Glia Biology*, 1(4): 351–363.

Kahneman, D (2011). *Thinking Fast and Slow*. New York: Farrar, Straus and Giroux.

Karbach, J. & Schubert, T. (2013). Training-induced cognitive and neural plasticity. *Frontiers in Human Neuroscience*, 7(48): 1–2.

Kaufman, S. B. (2009). Love, lust, and creativity. *Psychology Today*. Retrieved January 5, 2018 from: www.psychologytoday.com/blog/beautiful-minds/200909/love-lust-and-creativity

(2010). Why creative folks blink a lot. *Psychology Today*. Retrieved July 10, 2018 from: www.psychologytoday.com/blog/beautiful-minds/201004/why-creative-folks-blink-lot

(2013). The real neuroscience of creativity. *Scientific American*. Retrieved June 1, 2018 from: https://blogs.scientificamerican.com/beautiful-minds/the-real-neuroscience-of-creativity/

Kenney, P. (2001). Framing, political opportunities, and civic mobilization in the eastern European revolutions: A case study of Poland's freedom and peace movement. *Mobilization*, 6(2): 193–210.

(2008). *A Carnival of Revolution: Central Europe 1989*. Princeton, NJ: Princeton University Press.

Kim, W. C. & Mauborgne, R. (2005). *Blue Ocean Strategy: How to Create Uncontested Market Space and Make Competition Irrelevant*. Cambridge, MA: Harvard Business Review Press.

Kirkpatrick, D. (2011). *Beyond Empowerment: The Age of the Self-Managed Organization*. Sacramento, CA: Morning Star Self-Management Institute.

Klemm, B. (2008). New neurons: Good news, bad news. *SharpBrains*. Retrieved September 7, 2018 from: https://sharpbrains.com/blog/2008/04/25/new-neurons-good-news-bad-news/

Koestler, A. (2009). The three domains of creativity. In: Krausz, M. & Dutton, D. (Eds.), *The Idea of Creativity* (pp. 251–266). Leiden, Netherlands: Brill.

Kogon, C. (2013). Dance as a tool for creativity with young people. *Tools for Learning*. Retrieved April 10, 2018 from: http://educationaltoolsportal.eu/en/tools-for-learning/dance-tool-creativity-young-people

Kramer, A. F., Bherer, L., Colcombe, S. J., William, W. D., & Greenough, W. T. (2004). Environmental influences on cognitive and brain plasticity during aging. *Journals of Gerontology*, 59(9): M940–M957.

Krumrie, M. (2014). How to deal with employee personal issues in the workplace. *ZipRecruiter*. Retrieved June 5, 2017 from: www.ziprecruiter.com/blog/employee-personal-issues-in-workplace/

Lakoff, G. & Johnson, M. (2003). *Metaphors We Live By*. Chicago, IL: University of Chicago Press.

Lange, A. (2016). The innovation campus: Building better ideas. *New York Times*. Retrieved November 6, 2017 from: www.nytimes.com/2016/08/07/education/edlife/innovation-campus-entrepreneurship-engineering-arts.html

Leeds-Hurwitz, W. (2009). Social construction of reality. In: Littlejohn, S. & Foss, K. (Eds.), *Encyclopedia of Communication Theory* (pp. 892–895). Thousand Oaks, CA: SAGE.

Lindsay, G. (2014). Engineering serendipity. Aspen Ideas Festival. Retrieved July 10, 2018 from: https://medium.com/aspen-ideas/engineering-serendipity-941e601a9b65#.eicshe5kn

Machik, J. L. (2000). Educational differences between inner-city classrooms and suburban classrooms. University of Delaware, EDUC258.00S: Cultural Diversity. Retrieved June 29, 2017 from: http://ematusov.soe.udel.edu/final.paper.pub/_pwfsfp/00000002.htm

Maguire, E. A., Woollett, K., & Spiers H. J. (2006). London taxi drivers and bus drivers: A structural MRI and neuropsychological analysis. *Hippocampus*, 16(12): 1091–1101.

Maguire, E. A., Gadian, D. G., Johnsrude, I. S., Good, C. D., Ashburner, J., Frackowiak, R. S. J., & Frith, C. D. (2000). Navigation-related structural change in the hippocampi of taxi drivers. *PNAS, Proceedings of the National Academy of Sciences of the United States of America*, 97(8): 4398–4403.

Majd, S. (2012). *How to Live with a Young Brain?* Melbourne: Amazon Australia Services.

Mapes, J. J. (2003). *Quantum Leap Thinking*. Naperville, IL: Sourcebooks.

Maresco, P. A. & York, C. C. (2005). Ricardo Semler: Creating organizational change through employee empowered leadership. Resource document. *Academic Leadership Online Journal*. Retrieved January 31, 2017 from: www.newunionism.net/library/case%20studies/SEMCO%20-%20Employee-Powered%20Leadership%20-%20Brazil%20-%202005.pdf

Marsh, D. R., Schroeder, D. G., Dearden, K. A., Sternin, J., & Sternin, M. (2004). The power of positive deviance. *British Medical Journal*, 13(329/7475): 1177–1179.

Maslow, A. H. (1943). A theory of human motivation. *Psychological Review*, 50(4): 370–396.

Mastin, L. (2018). The human memory. Retrieved July 9, 2018 from: www.human-memory.net/brain_neurons.html

McChrystal, S. (2015). *Team of Teams: New Rules of Engagement for a Complex World*. New York: Portfolio.

McFadzean, E. (1998). Enhancing creative thinking within organizations. *Management Decision*, 36(5): 309–315.

McGoldrick, M. & Gerson, R. (1985). *Genograms in Family Assessment*. New York: W. W. Norton & Co.

McLeod, S. (2007). Moscovici and minority influence. *Simply Psychology*. Retrieved July 9, 2018 from: www.simplypsychology.org/minority-influence.html

McWeeny, K. H., Young, A. W., Hay, D. C., & Ellis, A. W. (1987). Putting names to faces. *British Journal of Psychology*, 78(2): 143–149.

Mechelli, A., Crinion, J. T., Noppeney, U., O'Doherty, J., Ashburner, J., Frackowiak, R. S., & Price, C. J. (2004). Neurolinguistics: Structural plasticity in the bilingual brain. *Nature*, 431(7010): 757.

Michelon, P. (2008). Brain plasticity: How learning changes your brain. *SharpBrains*. Retrieved September 7, 2018 from https://sharpbrains.com/blog/2008/02/26/brain-plasticity-how-learning-changes-your-brain/

Miller, L. M. (2013). Dr. Deming's joy at work, happiness & the high performance organization. *IndustryWeek*. Retrieved April 5, 2018 from: www.industryweek.com/engagement/dr-demings-joy-work-happiness-high-performance-organization

Moreno, S., Marques, C., Santos, A., Santos, M., Castro, S. L., & Besson, M. (2008). Musical training influences linguistic abilities in 8-year-old children: More evidence for brain plasticity. *Cerebral Cortex*, 19(3): 712–723.

Morosini, P. (2010). *Seven Keys to Imagination: Creating the Future by Imagining the Unthinkable and Delivering It*. London: Marshall Cavendish.

Morreal, J. (2001). Humor in the Holocaust: Its critical, cohesive, and coping functions. Holocaust Teacher Resource Center. Retrieved March 22, 2018 from: www.holocaust-trc.org/humor-in-the-holocaust/

Morrens, J., Van Den Broeck, W., & Kempermann, G. (2012). Glial cells in adult neurogenesis. *Glia*, 60(2): 159–174.

Moscovici, S. (1976). *Social Influence and Social Change*. London: Academic Press.

Moskowitz, G. B. (2005). *Social Cognition: Understanding Self and Others*. New York: Guilford Press.

Naccache, P., Leca, B., & Kazmi, B. A. (2017). Corporate social responsibility: The need for a bottom-up approach. *European Financial Review*. Retrieved July 9, 2018 from: www.europeanfinancialreview.com/?p=12786

Nazemoff, V. (2015). 6 steps to "dancing" through conversations with your business partners. *Entrepreneur*. Retrieved April 11, 2018 from: www.entrepreneur.com/article/247971

(2017). *The Dance of the Business Mind*. Stabio, Switzerland: TI Press.

Nemeth, C. J. & Goncalo, J. A. (2005). Influence and persuasion in small groups. In: Brock, T. C. & Green, M. C. (Eds.), *Persuasion: Psychological Insights and Perspectives* (pp. 171–194). Thousand Oaks, CA: Sage.

Neumeier, M. (2014). 6 changes that will make you more imaginative. *FastCompany*. Retrieved May 31, 2018 from: www.fastcompany.com/3028296/6-changes-that-will-make-you-more-imaginative

Nichols, M. P. (1984). *Family Therapy: Concepts and Methods*. New York: Gardner Press.

Nieto, M. J. & Santamaría, L. (2007). The importance of diverse collaborative networks for the novelty of product innovation. *Technovation*, 27(6–7): 367–377.

Nowak, A. & Vallacher, R. R. (2005). Information and influence in the construction of shared reality. *IEEE: Intelligent Systems*, 1: 90–93.

Osa, M. (2003). *Solidarity and Connections: Networks of Polish Opposition.* Minneapolis: University of Minnesota Press.

Oswalt, A. (2010). Erik Erikson and self-identity. MentalHelp.net. Retrieved July 9, 2018 from: www.mentalhelp.net/articles/erik-erikson-and-self-identity/

Otte, A. (2001). The plasticity of the brain. *European Journal of Nuclear Medicine*, 28(3): 263–265.

Pascual-Leone, A., Amedi, A., Fregni, F., & Merabet, L. B. (2005). The plastic human brain cortex. *Annual Review of Neuroscience*, 28: 377–401.

Pascual-Leone, A., Freitas, C., Oberman, L., Horvath, J. C., Halko, M., Eldaief, M., et al. (2011). Characterizing brain cortical plasticity and network dynamics across the age-span in health and disease with TMS-EEG and TMS-fMRI. *Brain Topography*, 24: 302–315.

Pawłowski, P. (2009). My way to integration. Retrieved May 10, 2017 from: www .niepelnosprawni.pl/ledge/x/52975

Pellis, S. & Pellis, V. (2009). *The Playful Brain: Venturing to the Limits of Neuroscience.* London: Oneworld Publications.

Pérez, A., Carreiras, M., & Duñabeitia, J. A. (2017). Brain-to-brain entrainment: EEG interbrain synchronization while speaking and listening. *Scientific Reports*, 7(4190). Retrieved July 10, 2018 from: www.nature.com/articles/ s41598-017-04464-4

Porter, J. (2014). The neuroscience of imagination. *Forbes*. Retrieved May 31, 2018 from: www.fastcompany.com/3026510/the-neuroscience-of-imagination

Powers, R. (2010). Use it or lose it: Dancing makes you smarter, longer. Stanford Dance. Retrieved April 13, 2018 from: https://socialdance.stanford.edu/ syllabi/smarter.htm

Praszkier, R. (2012). Social entrepreneurs open closed worlds: The transformative influence of weak ties. In: Nowak, A., Winkowska-Nowak, K., & Bree, D. (Eds.), *Complex Human Dynamics, From Mind to Societies* (pp. 111–129). New York: Springer.

(2014). Empathy, mirror neurons and SYNC. *Mind & Society*, 15(1): 1–25.

(2018). *Empowering Leadership of Tomorrow.* New York: Cambridge University Press.

(2019). What makes profound and peaceful social transitions? A case of solidarity: The Polish underground movement. iASK Polányi Centre Publications, II.2018/WP01.

Praszkier, R. & Nowak, A. (2012). *Social Entrepreneurship: Theory and Practice.* New York: Cambridge University Press.

Praszkier, R., Nowak, A., & Coleman, P. (2010). Social entrepreneurs and constructive change: The wisdom of circumventing conflict. *Peace and Conflict: Journal of Peace Psychology*, 16: 153–174.

Putnam, R. D. (1993). The prosperous community: Social capital and public life. *American Prospect*, 13: 35–42.

Raymond, E. S. (2001). *The Cathedral & the Bazaar: Musings on Linux and Open Source by an Accidental Revolutionary.* Sebastopol, CA: O'Reilly Media.

Reddish, P., Fischer, R., & Bulbulia, J. (2013). Let's dance together: Synchrony, shared intentionality and cooperation. *PLoS One*, 8(8): e71182.

Robbins, A. (1997). *Unlimited Power: The New Science of Personal Achievement*. New York: Free Press.

Roberts, R. M. (1989). *Serendipity: Accidental Discoveries in Science*. Somerset, NJ: John Wiley & Sons.

Rogers, C. (1995). *On Becoming a Person: A Therapist's View of Psychotherapy*. New York: Houghton Mifflin.

Rosenberg McKay, D. (2016). How to deal with personal issues at work. *TheBalance*. Retrieved July 9, 2018 from: www.thebalance.com/how-to-deal-with-personal-issues-at-work-526107

Rubin, R. D., Watson, P. D., Duff, M. C., & Cohen, N. J. (2014). The role of the hippocampus in flexible cognition and social behavior. *Frontiers in Human Neuroscience*, 8(742): 1–15.

Runco, M. A. (2007). *Creativity. Theories and Themes: Research, Development and Practice*. Burlington: Elsevier Academic Press.

Russ, S. W. (2003). Play and creativity: Developmental issues. *Scandinavian Journal of Educational Research*, 47(3): 291–303.

Rusu, I. (2013). Dopamine, endorphins and epinephrine. *European Journal of Science and Theology*, 9(6): 1–3.

Sacks, O. (1998). *A Leg to Stand On*. New York: Touchstone.

Sale, A., Berardi, N., & Maffei, L. (2014). Environment and brain plasticity: Towards an endogenous pharmacotherapy. *Physiological Reviews*, 94(1): 189–234.

Sandstrom, G. M. & Dunn, E. W. (2014). The surprising power of weak ties. *Personality and Social Psychology Bulletin*, 40(7): 910–922.

Sanow, A. (2015). "Sync" into others to build connect-ability and rapport. *Leader's Beacon*. Retrieved July 10, 2018 from: www.leadersbeacon.com/sync-into-others-to-build-connect-ability-and-rapport/

Santos, R. G., Chartier, M. J., Whalen, J. C., Chateau, D., & Boyd, L. (2011). Effectiveness of school-based violence prevention for children and youth: Cluster randomized field trial of the Roots of Empathy program with replication and three-year follow-up. *Healthcare Quarterly*, 14: 80–90.

Sarris, M. (2015). The stigma of autism: When all eyes are upon you. Interactive Autism Network. Retrieved July 8, 2017 from: https://iancommunity.org/ssc/autism-stigma

Scheve, T. (2014). What are endorphins? *How Stuff Works; Science*. Retrieved July 10, 2018 from: http://science.howstuffworks.com/life/endorphins1.htm

Schonert-Reichl, K. A., Smith, V., Zaidman-Zait, A., & Hertzman, C. (2012). Promoting children's prosocial behaviours in school: Impact of the "Roots of Empathy" program on the social and emotional competence of school-aged children. *School Mental Health*, 4(1): 1–12.

Schwartz, B. (2012). *Rippling: How Social Entrepreneurs Spread Innovation Throughout the World*. San Francisco, CA: Jossey-Bass.

Scott, W. A. (1962). Cognitive complexity and cognitive flexibility. *Sociometry. American Sociological Association*, 25(4): 405–414.

Seethamraju, R. (2011). Enhancing student learning of enterprise integration and business process orientation through an ERP business simulation game ERP – enterprise resource planning. *Journal of Information Systems Education*, 22(1): 19–29.

Semler, R. (1994). Why my former employees still work for me. *Harvard Business Review*. Retrieved January 31, 2017 from: https://hbr.org/1994/01/why-my-former-employees-still-work-for-me

(1995). *Maverick: The Success Story Behind the World's Most Unusual Workplace*. New York: Warner Books.

(2004). *The Seven-Day Weekend: Changing the Way Work Works*. New York: Portfolio.

Shapira, O. & Liberman, N. (2009). An easy way to increase creativity. *Scientific American*. Retrieved June 1, 2018 from: www.scientificamerican.com/article/an-easy-way-to-increase-c

Shelton, C. D. (2013). *Brain Plasticity: Rethinking How the Brain Works*. London, Canada: Choice PH.

Smith, G. E., Housen, P., Yaffe, K., Ruff, R., Kennison, R. F., Mahncke, H. W., & Zelinski, E. M. (2009). A cognitive training program based on principles of brain plasticity: Results from the improvement in memory with plasticity-based adaptive cognitive training (IMPACT) study. *Journal of the American Geriatrics Society*, 57(4): 594–603.

Smith, S. (2016). Presenteeism costs business 10 times more than absenteeism. *EHS Today*. Retrieved July 9, 2018 from: www.ehstoday.com/safety-leadership/presenteeism-costs-business-10-times-more-absenteeism

Sporns, O. (2016). *Discovering the Human Connectome*. Cambridge, MA: MIT Press.

Sporns, O., Tononi, G., & Kötter, R. (2005). The human connectome: A structural description of the human brain. *PLoS Computational Biology*, 1(4): e42.

Sprouse-Blum, A. S, Smith, G., Sugai, D., & Parsa, F. D. (2010). Understanding endorphins and their importance in pain management. *Hawaii Medical Journal*, 69(3): 70–71.

Sternin, J. (2002). Positive deviance: A new paradigm for addressing today's problems today. *Journal of Corporate Citizenship*, 5: 57–62. Retrieved December 19, 2017 from: www.highbeam.com/doc/1G1-84669002 .html

Stoppler, M. C. (2014). Endorphins: Natural pain and stress fighters. MedicineNet.com. Retrieved July 10, 2018 from: www.medicinenet.com/script/main/art.asp?articlekey=55001

Strickland, B. & Rause, V. (2009). *Make the Impossible Possible: One Man's Crusade to Inspire Others to Dream Bigger and Achieve the Extraordinary*. New York: Broadway Books.

Strogatz, S. (2003). *Sync: How Order Emerges from Chaos in the Universe, Nature, and Daily Life*. New York: Hyperion.

Talbot, P. A. (2003). Corporate generals: The military metaphor of strategy. *Irish Journal of Management*, 24(2): 1–10.

Taleb, N. N. (2010). *The Black Swan: The Impact of the Highly Improbable*. New York: Random House.

Tallat, N., Fatima, A., Fiza, K., & Adiya, D. (2017). Body's image concerns and its impact on academic achievements. *Journal of Psychology and Clinical Psychiatry*, 7(3): 1–250.

Toynbee, A. (1962). Has America neglected her creative minorities? *Sooner Magazine*, January 1962: 7–9. Retrieved October 15, 2017 from: https://digital.libraries.ou.edu/sooner/articles/p7-9_1962v34n5_OCR.pdf

Trayford, M. (2014). 3 real life examples of brain plasticity. APEX Brain Centers. Retrieved July 9, 2018 from: http://apexbraincenters.com/blog/3-real-life-examples-of-brain-plasticity/

Trope, Y. & Liberman, N. (2010). Construal-level theory of psychological distance. *Psychological Review*, 117(2): 440–463.

Uhlig, D. K. (n.d.). Importance of diagonal communication routes. *Small Business – Chron.com*. Retrieved July 10, 2018 from http://smallbusiness.chron.com/importance-diagonal-communication-routes-35496.html

UN Rights Experts (2015). Discrimination against autistic persons, the rule rather than the exception. United Nations Human Rights Office of the High Commissioner. Retrieved July 9, 2018 from: www.ohchr.org/EN/NewsEvents/Pages/DisplayNews.aspx?NewsID=15787

Valdesolo, P. & DeSteno, D. (2011). Synchrony and the social tuning of compassion. *Emotion*, 11(2): 262–266.

Vallacher, R. R. & Nowak, A. (2007). Dynamical social psychology: Finding order in the flow of human experience. In: Kruglanski, A. W. & Higgins, E. T. (Eds.), *Social Psychology: Handbook of Basic Principles* (pp. 734–758). New York: Guilford Publications.

von Oech, R. (2008). *A Whack on the Side of the Head: How You Can Be More Creative*. New York: Warner Books.

Wagner, J. & Watch, D. (2017). Innovation spaces: The new design of work. Brookings. Retrieved July 10, 2018 from: www.brookings.edu/research/innovation-spaces-the-new-design-of-work/

Watzlawick, P. (1997). *How Real Is Real?* London: Vintage.

Wells, D. E. (2018). From social entrepreneurship to everyone a changemaker: 40 years of social innovation point to what's next. *Social Innovations Journal*, 52. Retrieved December 4, 2018 from: https://socialinnovationsjournal.org/editions/issue-52/75-disruptive-innovations/2906-from-social-entrepreneurship-to-everyone-a-changemaker-40-years-of-social-innovation-point-to-what-s-next?mc_cid=83db5c2cda&mc_eid=5e96e1f8dc

Wilk, J. (1985). This reminds me of a story. *Family Therapy Networker*, 9(2): 45–48.

Wiltermuth, S. S. & Heath, C. (2009). Synchrony and cooperation. *Psychological Science*, 20(1): 1–5.

Woolcock, M. & Narayan, D. (2000). Social capital: Implications for development; theory, research, and policy. *World Bank Research Observer*, 15(2): 225–249.

Yun, K., Watanabe, K., & Shimojo, S. (2012). Interpersonal body and neural synchronization as a marker of implicit social interaction. *Scientific Reports*, 2(959): 1–8.

Yunus, M. (2003). *Banker to the Poor: The Story of the Grameen Bank*. London: Aurum Press.

Index